Selected Poems

Talking Pictures

Riemke Ensing

With an Introduction
by Lawrence Jones

HEADWORX
WELLINGTON

First published 2000

ISBN 0-473-06804-4

Published by

HeadworX Publishers
26 Grant Rd, Thorndon
Wellington
Aotearoa / New Zealand
http://headworx.eyesis.co.nz

Printed by

Publishing Press

HeadworX® is a registered
trademark of HeadworX Publishers

Typeset by HeadworX Publishers
in Guatemala 11pt

Selected Poems
Talking Pictures

Also by Riemke Ensing

Poetry

Making / Inroads

Letters

Topographies

Spells from Chagall

The 'K.M.' File

Like I have seen the dark green ladder climbing

Dear Mr Sargeson ...

Finding the Ancestors

Tarawera — Te Maunga Tapu

Edited

Private Gardens

Poetry NZ 5

Gloria — In Excelsis

Art Criticism

Stanley Palmer : Poor Knights

This book has been published with
a grant from Creative NZ/Toi Aotearoa

creative nz
Arts Council of New Zealand Toi Aotearoa

Gingko

Leaf enclosed in
a letter to my mother

This is a leaf
on a twig of a branch
from a tree
thought to be the oldest
in the world
and I send it to you
to cure your winter cold.

Acknowledgements

Many of these poems have been previously published in the following magazines and anthologies:

Alumni News (The University of Auckland), *An Anthology of New Zealand Poetry in English* (Oxford), *An Anthology of Twentieth Century New Zealand Poetry* (Oxford), *Antipodes New Writing, Ariel* (Canada), *Below the Surface, Climate, Countless Signs, Descant* (Canada), *Doors, Earth Against Heaven* (Australia), *15 Contemporary New Zealand Poets, Hecate* (Australia), *Inheriting the Netherlands – A Century of Dutch Art in New Zealand, JAAM, Jewels in the Water, Kite, Kiwi & Emu* (Australia), *Kunapipi* (Denmark), *Landfall, Listener, Maatstaf* (Netherlands), *Mate, Meanjin* (Australia), *New Canadian Review* (Canada), *New Directions* (USA), *New Zealand Author, Older & Bolder, Penguin Book of Contemporary New Zealand Poetry, Poems by Several Hands, Poetry New Zealand, Poetry NZ, Printout, Rambling Jack, Sites* (USA), *Southern Review* (Australia), *SPAN, Spin, Takahe, The Visionary, Thylazine* (Australia), *Vital Writing 1, Whales – A Celebration* and *Yellow Pencils.*

Poems have also been selected from: *Letters* (The Lowry Press, 1982), *Topographies* (Prometheus Press, 1984), *Spells from Chagall* (The Griffin Press, 1987), *The 'K.M.' File* (Hazard Press, 1993), *Like I have seen the dark green ladder climbing* (The Pear Tree Press, 1995), *Dear Mr Sargeson ...* (Cape Catley, 1995), *Finding the Ancestors* (The Pear Tree Press, 1999), and *Tarawera – Te Maunga Tapu* (The Pear Tree Press, 1999). Thanks are due to the publishers.

The drawing which accompanies 'Crossings' is 'Ko to pukapuka o te Tarakona, 19 November 1855', Kenneth Webster papers, MS-Group 002, Alexander Turnbull Library.

The picture on p. 71 is a detail from a photo by David Moore, 'Migrants Arriving in Sydney'.

Cover image adapted from 'The Tree of the Soul', figure by William Law from *The Works of Jacob Boehme*, London, 1764-81.

Special thanks to Mark Pirie for his editorial assistance.

Contents

From *The 'K.M.' File*

What Shall We Tell Li Po: Poems for China

Kirikau

From *Dear Mr Sargeson ...*

Introduction

Riemke Ensing's background is unusual among New Zealand writers and has had a profound effect on her poetry. Born in Groningen, the Netherlands in 1939, she and her family arrived in New Zealand in 1951, part of that influx of 10,000 Dutch immigrants between 1950 and 1953, leaving behind them World War Two and its aftermath and searching for a better life in a new world. She had no English when she arrived, but soon was so proficient that she became a teacher after attending Ardmore Training College, and later joined the staff there as a lecturer. A move to the English Department at the University of Auckland, where at first she was seeking a higher degree, led to her long career as Senior Tutor, specialising in New Zealand literature. During these years she gradually built up a rich body of published poetry.

She first came to public notice in 1977 as editor of *Private Gardens,* the first substantial New Zealand anthology of poetry by women, while in 1979 she read *Making / Inroads* as an invocation at the New Zealand Women's Convention in Hamilton (it was published as a pamphlet in 1980). Her work had also been appearing in a variety of periodicals since the late 1960s, but the first collection, *Letters,* did not appear till 1982. It was soon followed by the long poem *Topographies* (1984) and *Spells from Chagall* (1987), and by a flurry of publication in the 1990s: *The 'K. M.' File and other poems with Katherine Mansfield* (1993), *Like I have seen the dark green ladder climbing* and *Dear Mr Sargeson ...* (both 1995), and two elegantly produced booklets in 1999, *Finding the Ancestors* and *Tarawera — Te Maunga Tapu.* Her work was also featured by Alistair Paterson in *Poetry NZ* issue 9 (a magazine that Ensing edited herself for issue 5), and she has edited and introduced *Gloria — In Excelsis* (1995), a selection from the poems of Gloria Rawlinson. Her poems have appeared in anthologies in New Zealand, Australia, the Netherlands, Canada, India and the US.

A career then, and a surprising one. I can remember Charles Brasch once saying that you could not get a good cup of coffee in Dunedin until the Dutch came (and I think of my first cup of Kiwi coffee, an undrinkable liquid made up from an unspeakable concoction known as 'coffee and chicory essence', as against the real coffee served by a

Dutch friend), and I remember the Dutch herb cheese at Wardell's when the only New Zealand cheeses were 'mild', 'medium' and 'tasty' — cheddar, of course, and the Dutch butcher who made salami when the standard sandwich fare was fat, bland, artificially coloured 'Belgian sausage'. The Dutch contribution to New Zealand society was pretty immediately evident, even to an American immigrant. But poetry? The visual arts maybe, but Ensing and Koenraad Kuiper are the only writers named in the entry under 'Netherlands, The' in *The Oxford Companion to New Zealand Literature* (1998). Perhaps this is why Ensing's poetry is unique, impossible to classify in any of the usual categories. The counterculture of the *Freed* group who paralleled Ensing's emergence in the late 1960s/early 1970s seems irrelevant to her work, as does Curnow's and Baxter's work (although she has written well of Baxter's). Despite *Private Gardens* and her friendship with some of the poets themselves, her work does not fit in easily with the new women's poetry that arose in the mid-70s (as was perhaps indicated in the puzzled response to *Making / Inroads*), although no reader could mistake its gender origin. Despite her inclusion in Alistair Paterson's *15 Contemporary New Zealand Poets* (1980) and in his later mini-anthology in *New Directions*, she cannot be characterised as a typical 'open former', although her verse has its share of ampersands and slashes and is typographically adventurous. Perhaps this is why David Eggleton more usefully refers to her not in terms of group/genre loyalties but rather as a 'thorny individualist' and her books as 'idiosyncratic' (in *Landfall* 190). Ensing has her own voice and eye and frame of reference in her poetry, and the Dutch origins are a significant factor in this uniqueness, contributing a European quality which has made an increasingly rich mix with a range of New Zealand (and other) elements.

In such early poems as 'Conversations for Miro' and 'Fires from Chagall' (collected in *Letters* in 1982 and then in 1985 presented as one poem in the prestigious US annual, *New Directions* 49), the European elements are dominant — the references to the painters, the highly visual quality, with the images surreal, dream-like, related to those in paintings. There is little that is literal in the realist mode, but there are strong appeals to the senses, and a concern for the limitations of language in trying to deal with the subjective experience of them, as in 'Conversations for Miro' where a dictionary definition of 'persimmon' is incorporated into the poem and paradoxically juxtaposed to words pointing to an experience beyond words:

go and see the tree
put the fruit in your hand, your mouth
mix shape and form with what
you feel and see and mostly touch
and smell or taste and hear.

If the imagery can sometimes be rather private in its implications, too rich in its profusion to cohere, as in 'Fires from Chagall', nonetheless individual passages may glow for the reader.

'Inheritors', from the same volume, shows the New Zealand elements entering in — New Zealand places, Maori experience, the old Maori woman's diary — a text like Ensing's own poems in capturing a subtle, fragile subjectivity of impressions:

... the diary
where the old lady spun her web
of words fragile as dawn on dew
in a valley where all sound is a twist
of wind as it curls
up the beach ....

A few years later in *Topographies* (1984) the European and New Zealand elements are consciously brought together:

Meaning & memory pieced together, drawing lines
from here to there and back
again ...

Ensing has called the book her 'first concentrated response to the fact of being a migrant', an 'attempt to piece together both the past and the present, the *here* with the *there*, connecting history, myth, and the fragmented details of two small parcels of earth on different sides of the world' (in 'Maps of the Heart' in *Migration and New Zealand Society: Proceedings of the Stout Research Centre Sixth Annual Conference 1990*). There are references to New Zealand places and history and monuments, and sections of map (similar to those in the work of her fellow Auckland tutor for some years, Kendrick Smithyman), but there is also a map of Groningen, and references to childhood war experiences there. In the free, associative structure (a technique foreshadowed by the Pound of the *Cantos* and the William Carlos Williams of *Paterson*), links are made between Hitler and Muldoon, the Spanish Civil War and the Springbok Tour and Steve Biko (part of a continuing interest in political concerns), and at the beginning there is Tasman, paralleled to the poet in the Groningen-New Zealand voyage, underlined in

Nigel Brown's illustration (in the original book), with the line from A to B cutting across the picture of Tasman and the Long White Cloud. This is a poetry of connections:

Thus threads are tied, connections made,
landscapes traversed and read quite easily.

It is also a map or at least a signpost to her further work:

The chart I have mapped is
by no means
finished.

The process of connection begun in these early volumes continues in the later ones, with the threads being even more diverse. In *Spells from Chagall* (1987) images from a European past mix with present scenes in New Zealand, references to Persian, Chinese and Japanese art, and images from the work of Helen Shaw, to whose memory the book is dedicated and to whom the poems are addressed. In Shaw, a New Zealander but married to a European photographer (memorialised in Ensing's 'In Camera') and eclectic in her interests, she found a writer whose mode approximated her own, not only in its wide and multicultural range of reference, but in its fragile impressionism and its use of dream images:

Helen, your blue leaves reached
me across pages
startled as frozen streams.
Among letters, words
many, your poem so fragile
surely
the ice would break
if one crossed.
('Blue Leaves Clapping')

As Jan Kemp has remarked of these poems, they 'have a somewhat fragmented and textured surface, as if their images are made of strokes and daubs of paint or segments of stained glass, which, on closer looking, reveal in vignettes of small imaged areas, places we can see or enter into'. Thus 'things seen are miniature and particular', with 'an intimacy and delicacy' (*SPAN* 25) — typical of the 'feminine' impressionist tradition. The attempt to make connections among and bring in associations (and explanations) concerning these impressions leads in this book not only to the marginal references first found in *Topographies* but also to endnotes, techniques which characterise much of her later verse.

In Katherine Mansfield Ensing found another kindred New Zealand writer with a strong European element and an impressionistic way of working: 'Reality lies / in how you see things.' From such details as 'the sunday-take-him-out-of-the-box / fox' from 'Miss Brill' the art takes shape, a series of subjective impressions, suggestive in the way that the details of a Frances Hodgkins still life suggest Mansfield to Ensing or the details of a painting of Elizabeth I suggest Mansfield to herself or Mansfield's signature suggests a Zen painting. Quotations from Mansfield's own writing (identified in marginal references), references to paintings of her (in the original book including prints of those by Margaret Lawlor-Bartlett) and dream images come together in a subtle, suggestive, and fragile art:

the blue scent
of life
fragile
on the open page.
('K.M. at Garsington')

If Helen Shaw and Katherine Mansfield gave Ensing predecessors in a New Zealand impressionist tradition that could incorporate European and Oriental elements (most evident in her own work in the later poems from Li Po and for Izumi) with New Zealand experience in a fragile art, what about that other, once-dominant tradition of New Zealand writing represented by Frank Sargeson, who recognised Mansfield's tradition but called it 'minor', and whose work would certainly not be deemed 'fragile'? *Dear Mr Sargeson ...* is the result of Ensing's determination to 'have it out with Sargeson', confront his spirit in his cottage as she had not confronted him in life. She was obviously not at ease there. The image of his house is not a Mansfieldian, delicate one: 'grey / as a weathership in heavy / swells coming off the road' ('lighthouse'). The books on his shelves are mostly by 'chaps', and mostly English, American, and New Zealand — little European, nothing Oriental. The room is bare and 'practical', 'startling as a still life / without chrysanthemums' ('life'). She wants to oil and burnish the wood surfaces, put a bunch of grapes on the bench:

An effect
you might not think
appropriate here where everything is
functional

and there's no sign of that
waiting for something ...
to happen under the vine by your door.
('bringing katherine mansfield to esmonde rd')

She wants to bring in 'a lotus-holding Buddha to sit next / a bowl flame orange with persimmons / stroked in the sun' ('detail'), or to turn the bare bach into a teahouse. She wants to arrange words and things as they 'might have been' but were not. She does find that the lenses in Sargeson's glasses fit her — 'At least we have that much / in common' ('contrived'). But she also imaginatively recreates some of the 'abundance' that was there in Sargeson's literary social occasions, 'the salon with a difference'. And she finds at least one congenial sense experience, a loquat in fruit:

... Ripe
& succulent, a thousand suns
at least to cheer the wintry day.
('a time for sowing')

And she carries pips to sow, and later observes seedlings 'reaching / for a splash of sun' in the shade of his tree ('now'). The meeting with that Sargeson who after all finally rejected Karl Wolfskehl and his European heritage ('overpowered, weighed down by so much civilisation', he said in *Sargeson*) is perhaps a stand-off, as implied by the ambiguous title of the poem 'mate' — a poem about chess, not about Sargesonian mateship.

Ensing's encounter with Sargeson, then, was very different from her union with Mansfield. His tradition was not hers. Yet she had already in a sense absorbed something of his tradition, as is strikingly evident in the sequence *Kirikau.* In a deserted soldier-settlement community not far from the King Country farm of Sargeson's beloved uncle, she conjures up that last-frontier way of life — the repressed war memories, the puritan work-ethic, the grim poverty, the loneliness, the violence and sudden death, the hard family life and the terrible toil of the women. The only thing fragile here is the 'web of past' in the fine lines on Bill's worn hands, and the imagery is not from dreams or paintings and is not richly sensuous, but rather harshly literal, as in 'Tawata I — Beginnings':

... they carried bags of flour, others
of salt, an axe, a shotgun and a 303 for pigs
and food.

The language is like that of Sargeson's narrators — 'Poor buggers. First fight their guts out / on some piece of land in France or

Africa ....' If the realism is not quite Sargeson's, and the existence of women is recognised more than in his work, the range of experience and the mode of presenting it are recognisably in the same tradition.

The later poems collected here for the first time tend to integrate Groningen and different aspects of New Zealand, the past and the present, inner and outer, often quite explicitly as in 'Here I give thanks to Mondrian & McCahon &' — any number of names from a variety of sources might follow that last ampersand. The concern with the visual arts evident in that poem is constant in her work, there from the earliest poems and most directly expressed in her prose art criticism, but increasingly the references to European (and Asian) art are integrated with New Zealand references. A similar integration of European and New Zealand experience is evident in such poems as 'Finding the Ancestors', 'Labour Day — New Zealand', 'Naming', 'Interior', or 'Fictions', where the mythical 'remembered' tiles of Groningen blend with Mangawhare 'where all the roofs are tin'. Or, in 'A Whale in Auckland', where Greenpeace anti-whaling protests, *Moby-Dick*, Maui, and Jonah come together on Queen Street. Or in shorter poems where an image or a few related images will be developed, the source perhaps a European painter, Picasso or Matisse, or a photograph of a Dutch scene, or a New Zealand beach with 'the sand skimming across the dunes' ('Track with Tide Coming In') or a building on the 'corner of Grey / and Mayoral Drive' (Northern Building Society Office ...'). In structure the poems range from the haiku-like simplicity of 'Age' to the postmodern 'JOURNEY / going home' with its urban and suburban scenery and signs and brand-names, its casual references to Don Binney and Brent Wong and William Carlos Williams, its tricksy arrangement on the page — both sequential and simultaneous. With its refrain of *'going home'*, it is very much a poem by someone who in spite of constant reference to her Dutch origins is now at home in Auckland, carrying a richly mixed heritage within her, and responding to postmodern New Zealand society with her own way of seeing and saying.

Lawrence Jones
Dunedin
March-April 2000

CONVERSATIONS FOR MIRO

Conversations for Miro

the drawing in the poem / the poem in the drawing

I
Signs and patterns are what is common.
That line might be a flock of birds
migrating, could be the first stroke
towards saying I've changed my mind
not liking trickery, the games we play
the line we draw elaborately across
time forgetting the magic of colour and the sun
going down red over the horizon
in one fell swoop being swept off
the edge of the world and you're left
completely in the dark as to where
you are going.

A painter might draw beside you
symbols of landscape recognisably centred
as cloud in the window of the neighbour's
house   not moving though the wind blows.
A tree perhaps to shape you by   its leaves
making any one of four seasons.
These signs we decipher. They tell
stories ripe as aubergine or persimmon
tall as any dictionary where treasure is
kept.

persimmon, n. diospyros kaki.
American date plum
yellow fruit becoming
sweet when softened
by frost / persimmon
native of China bright

fruits will hang on
the tree in winter /
persimmon deciduous
small native to Japan
can be in weeping
form attractive both
in leaf   and fruit
after leaves have
fallen / persimmon
grows 15 feet
persimmon dios divine.

So much for words lying
their way from one book to another
way of saying here are the words, they tell
me a thing or two mostly
they are not the sound I want
to hear the wind
in branches the sun orange lush
or persimmon / dios divine
the word has its limits
go and see the tree
put the fruit in your hand, your mouth
mix shape and form with what
you feel and see and mostly touch
and smell or taste and hear.

Let the poet draw circles
round the moon   the painter till
his garden, plant trees for us
to sit under and smile
as the wind does when it's up
to mischief and blows human flowers
into the book we could be.

II

These words are about lines scored
with burin or pen   how charcoal spirits
away the harsh imprint of winter engraved
needlesharp on the mind like poems
the lithographs of sound shaped
by a point fine as glass drawing
blood and the full crescendo of cathedral
music singing from the stained window
of the heart shaped as magic flame dressed
gayer than harlequin riding on rooster
or peacocks reaching for rainbows.

III

The poem I started is already
lost. One day I will find it
on a sheet of paper pulled out
from a pile of books or unanswered letters.
Perhaps it will be
a bookmark showing the way
to mushroom growing or porcelain
glazes delicate as the smudge of Puzzuoli
red in a sketch where nothing is
sentimental but all lives speak
clearly as words do when they cry
from the heart without design
or drama   plainly as a flight of birds caught
in the sharp magic of black surprising
with its coat of colours.

TARAWERA —
TE MAUNGA TAPU

For the painter Margaret Lawlor-Bartlett

Taonga

For the painter Margaret Lawlor-Bartlett

I see the mountain [Tarawera]
now
is no longer
outside.

It has entered this room
the window into your house
your body
a meeting place [James K. Baxter]
where colours sing *Jubilates*
and line exults to draw
the ancestors breathing
into these soaring
graphites and paints.

Tarawera: Wairua (essence)

The mountain
is autobiographical.
It is
itself.

The mountain is all
about us.

(*The mountain*
is all about us.)

We lift up our eyes
and it lies
within us
Kaitiaki / protector

['to the mountains from
whence cometh our help.'
Psalm 121:1]

and it is
itself
still.

In the painting
rumble is silence.
You cannot hear
the wind scraping,
scrabbling across scoria.

You see steam rise
and the sound of terror
the black stone of ancient blood.

A poem is not a mountain.
But a mountain is

music defining the sky's edge.

Distantly
spheres spiral [Plato]
and shells.

Tarawera: Night Mountain

A variation

The night is a slight fear
rustling reeds
over the pulse of waves.

A squall darker than time
lost swimming against currents
and the last warning still
screaming in the roof of the mouth [Edvard Munch]
of the mountain.

A single terror caught
in that upraised hand
drowning or waving [Stevie Smith]
in the tugging water.

A bird flits past
ruru
small shadow
taking your eye to the curve of light
singing the world awake. [Plato]

Te Maunga Tapu

Nothing can take the past
away. It grows as shadows
for shelter. The dead live
in winds, trees, the call of birds
settling in the shoulder of mountain.

Spirits turn landmarks
take form,
talk with us.

In the house of the ancestors
the heart's dark contour
beats its pattern of fire.

Birds Passing the Night

In the flight of the ruru
voices recalling the past
shaping the future perhaps
Ancestors
seating themselves at the window
glad to be part of the talk
the reverence for night
when wind blows us
stories and rain is a song
caught in the remembering throat.

The Painter's Studio at Tarawera

For Peter Bartlett, architect

In this house on the rim
of the lake upstaging
the mountain, windows delight
the stars and everywhere high domes
steady the elements of earth
and fire.
Here you excavate limits;
an architecture of curves drawing
its pleasure from the light
arching of palms spreading [Mamaku]
their arms in benediction.
Points are drawn
from earth to sky bathing
translucent in water. A construct
scaled to wonder a reach beyond
infinity. [Zen]
Concordare. Lines
resounding psalms of life.

TOPOGRAPHIES

In the meantime ashes
grow cold at my back and rain
closes the sky.

Meaning & memory pieced together,
drawing lines from here to there & back
again. A narration connecting parts
which make history, myth
and a small parcel of earth.

As for the door, it can be open or closed.

Topographies

ANAWHATA

[December 1981]

That ridge   the nose
of the Dogon mask carved
deep into shadows
you might see but take
for simple blackness
so stark the line, the dark striking
down the cliff where the fire
this summer has left

(scars)

the colour of the Bambara antelope
mask / blackened with red-hot iron
or nearer home, no doubt,
there are examples of what is black
and charred
and scraped.

Obsidian for instance. Certainly
this is violent country
and artifacts were found.
Adzes, weapons. Also fish
hooks and in another place
down at Takatu Point
a necklace of human teeth

Dogon mask: The desire to give tangible form to the spirit world as a means of gaining control over the creative force.

SITE NO: 229	GRID REF:
Q11 / 410688	99 3454

a skull, red hair and Huia
feathers.
Otherwise mostly midden, pits & pa.

Five or more pages of reference
and site locations
patiently fossicked.

X4 N 41/993510

Certainly there is that colour
in the records of death;
the names of graves inland
marked
by a picket fence,

and in the colour of the shipwrecks
on the bar.

Sunk:

the barque	*ORWELL*	1848
	H.M.S. ORPHEUS	1863
the cutter	*ELFIN QUEEN*	1865
	PROGRESS	1866
the barque	*CAMBODIA*	
the schooner	*CHALLENGE*	1870
	FLORA MACDONALD	
	& PAKU	

both cutters.

This list from *Ingram & Wheatley.*
As the tide swells, the ghost
of Hoturoa frothing
at the mouth
bares its white teeth
circles the canoe.

Off the inshore cliff
of Paratutae, a plaque
to mark the worst
disaster:

On February 7,1863, the steam corvette
H.M.S. ORPHEUS was wrecked entering
the Manukau Harbour. Of the 259 officers
and men there were 70 survivors.

---

187 dead where *'only gulls'* should dare
to play the doleful flute of wind.

Anawhata

Conversely, the names of streams — *Edward*
are friendly refrigerated water — *Smythe*
on dusty days tramping — *Trinity*
the Waitakeres. — *Perihi*

'Über allen Gipfeln ist Ruh'
but you note that *'the bird on*
the rock covered soon by
tide has no resting place.'

Goethe & Wiremu Kingi
meeting in the sun's slant
on the edge as it slips
into sky. Noah might even come
into it. On Ararat.

Fragments. Shapes.
A weave of patterns
sensing light & shade.

I have bought maps & books.
From *District Schemes* I try
to page some sense
of geography.

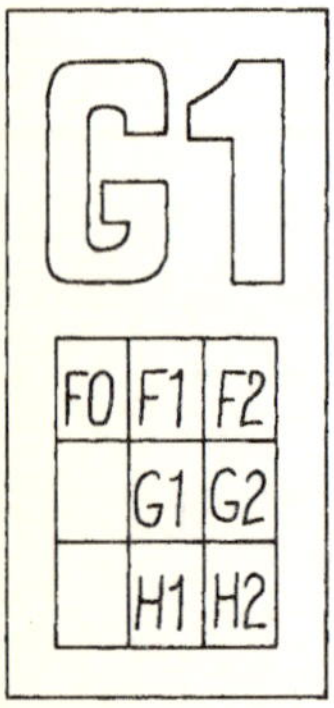

FO   Fl   G1
the direction itself a map.

The blank squares are sea.
The sections of the map
are joined on two lines.
I'm beginning to get the idea.

The tramping guide is adequate
only. I have the names of tracks,
a key to symbols as to where
things are.

That bird in flight
is a waterfall,
that little hat a beacon.

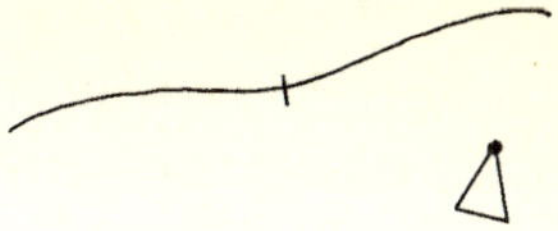

All the yellow is NO ENTRY
and at this point
I am 225 metres above sea-level.
I note we are at   Lat 35°55' South
                              Long 174°28' East
which means nothing to me
who knows little about maps
not having learned.   Coastlines
I can tramp. Directions
draw, being there.

I know where west is
because the sun's going down.

Here the road takes a bend
as in the picture Nigel sends
from my home town these 30 years
ago, where the water follows
the brick curve of centuries'
old walls and feet of warehouses.

'Ich hatte einst ein schones Vaterland',
goes the song in *Des Knaben Wunderhorn*
and had it been Russia it would be Mother
but as it is I fossick through whatever is
available to place myself / back there.

I point with some excitement to the lines
on a Baedeker (1897). Wasn't it
Eliot who mentioned him
also of the cigar? Appropriate then
that there should be my father's shop
(ENSING VOOR DE ROKER) bombed out
early (1940/41?) when I was small
and a child hiding under the table
in the Princessenweg, No. 8. (Tel 29001).

We'd go from here along Reitdiep
past the bridges, the granaries
into de Ouden Kijk in 't Jat straat
onto the Vismarkt and on
to the Grote Markt where on special days
you could pinch the fat lady for 6^d.

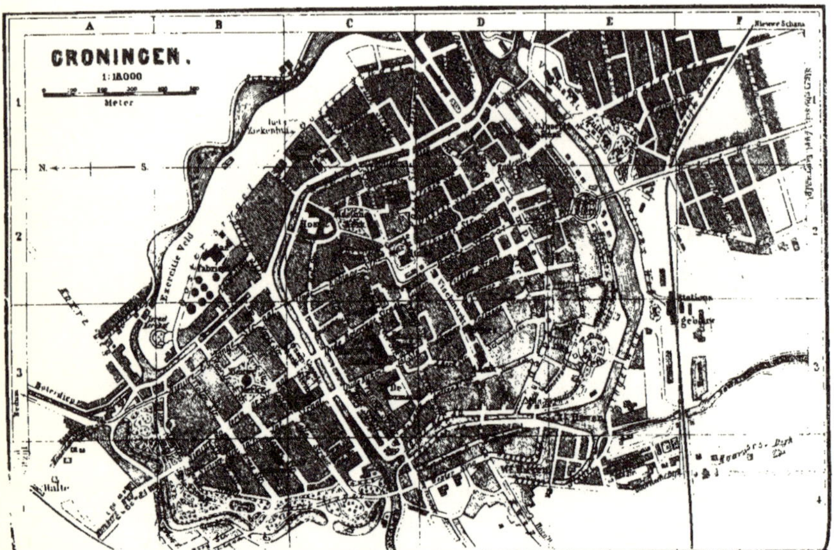

Quite purposefully the picture is vague.
How else to get you up there to the top
of the tower by winding staircase
to get a bird's eye view from the Martini
kerk / and make you lose
your stomach and your sense
as you sway holding on
for dear life and watch the moving
432 feet below for as long back as 1627.

The gate of the church opens in 1642,
Abel Tasman discovers Nieuw Zeeland
and Saskje van Uhlenburgh dies
leaving Rembrand. 340 years later
in Auckland a *still life with pomegranate*
and precious objects illumines the gallery
walls.

If you have a clue the message is simple
as a Chinese character. See how easy
it is / logical to open a door
you have two panels
the space is to walk through
or hang the branch of a tree
in moonlight.

門

Here then is the connection. This is where
fragments are severed by 340
years.
From the same town (more or less
give and take
a few miles)
to similar shores. From Zeehaan
and Heemskerk to an old troopship
converted and on its last voyage.

There was murder there too
because the dice fell skew.

So innocent rhymes connect histories,
make myths.

'Eie Wijkstra van Lutjegast
schoot zeven agenten door de ribbenkast.'
(And you note it was from behind a door.)

[29 June 1982]

In the fifth picture everything
turns from the centre to the corners
of the world where the scenes of life
are ... Zeehaan & Heemskerk coming
on *'a large land uplifted high*
in a fresh breeze on the wide open sea
rolling in huge swells.' The sky a billow
of parachute silk and the hills you will notice
change
with seasons / fall
of light, the way the sea shines
in the sky, the sky
on the water.

But I have turned away.

We were at Anawhata
where the road takes a bend
and straightens out into a curve
following the contour
of White's beach & buildings
are indicated.

There are six.
Of these I recognise four.

There is the architect's house,
the signal box, the painter's house
and a green garage
between macrocarpas
192 metres above mean sea
level / and yes, the sea can be
mean here.*

Already 5 drownings 32
rescues & various mishaps this season.

On the older map there are two houses.
Pine trees are also indicated.

Some things are constant
for a while.

Clouds scud past the moment-
ary sun. We are caught
up in the drift of things.

*ref. back

[17 January 1982]

This is the second Sunday after
Epiphany. You are locked in the sky
on your journey east. I'm walking
west into the sun. The hills leave
awesome shapes against the red.

There is someone down there
weaving on the loom of the sea.
The currents shoot back & forth
the undertow shuttles in three
directions to pattern a fabric
of terror & joy.

What do you think of the weaving ?
I ask James. From where I stand
the foam & water crashes
an amazing spread of crochet.
I like his image. He tells me
use it.

You note the Greeks keep appearing oddly
congruous in this landscape.
Penelope & Orpheus. The memories
of Odysseus haunting rock
and shadows. Something old
here. Older.

The poem has been held up
by domestic detail one might feel
at home with. The scraping of a door
back to the bare wood.
Uncovering it of layers of paint
discovering it in the fine gold
grain we call kauri.

This tells me nothing of giants
with heads green in the sky
so high. Nothing about twenty men
circling one tree and the saws
ripping for weeks before the tear /
ing timber scarred the hill, falling.

Nothing of that dreadful silence
after   and the burning.

May, 1772   *'We found enough timber in one tree to make a vessel of 74 guns.'**

*Thus the commander of the Marquis de Casties.

One tree to build a settlement /
church and all.

In our time / now we come
back to scale and a door
we've made a poem / going straight
to the heart of it / hard kauri
through endless surfaces
of grime, enamel. Stripped
it / ripped its vestments off it
one by one, revealing   [SS
history? Something about mythologies,   KKK
legends, folklore perhaps.   fascist]

On the panels, the first surface
in letters & words tell their own
story.
The usual.
Graffiti.

The scream of the thirties echoes
still round the sitting rooms
and Edvard Munch is alive & well
and hiding out in Ponsonby
where someone has painted
a message / also to make you laugh:

'Littler than Hitler but not so smart.'

Here the bootboys and brownshirts
took to the streets in '81
and Rouault's clown lies
bleeding in the bright hedge
of winter
still.

'Est par ses meurtrissures que nous
sommes gueris.'

'And with his stripes are we healed.'
(Isaiah 53:5)

Boarded windows
barbed wire
batons
BIKO boards
(All) Blacks

I carry an umbrella against the mood
of winter / and just in case.

Thus threads are tied, connections made,
landscapes traversed and read quite easily.

'I was conscious of what was happening
in the streets.' Federico

guarda / pistoles
sangre
muerto
despedida
(Farewell)

A page of figures to be filed
away.

In these grey times
Don Quixote de la Mancha
help us.

Small perplexities vex
the mind. I cross & recross
known paths and get lost
in the going. Always the coming
is being a spectator
at your own funeral. I follow
the journey in whatever direction
searching for what is forgotten
and the door might never again open
to worlds wrapped in grey cloaks
of mist and desolate winters

[1939-45]

where windows were blue / glass
painted against light. It was forever
dark. When planes fly over now I expect
the small green acre to be lit
up like Guy Fawkes night in a shower
of rockets & whizzbangs
shuddering & screeching their zig-zag
leaps & bounds across some plotted blue-
print path in Tommy Doo's office / corner
of Hobson & Cook among the bandaged

windows / while the night prowls
into the heart of dead theatre
tickets, and the insolent moon
climbs the narrow fire escape.

[1644] *'Aan dit kruis heeft men een tinnen schotel*
gevonden.'

Entries of lineage: gestures of history.

I travel through almanacs, catalogues
streets glimpsing nostalgia. Today
a find between the thin blue
cover of a library addition; Bruggenkate,
Karel, ten, (Groningen) 1849 — a dictionary
and an old friend filed at 439.313
B89.
I feel I could almost pay him
a visit. I write these lines towards
dusk on the other side of the world.
The door is open. A slight smell of winter
sweet exchanges wordless greetings,
casts a spell.

On that same door, under
the beading the brush has left
undamaged another tale.

$$\begin{array}{c} 6\,{}^{1}/_{2} \\ 7 \\ \hline 1.7\,{}^{1}/_{2} \end{array} \qquad\qquad \begin{array}{c} 3.6 \\ 2.3 \\ 2.7\,{}^{1}/_{2} \\ \hline 7.4\,{}^{1}/_{2} \end{array}$$

Legends carpenters might read
and intrigue us.

As the poem has waited for the door
so the hills here also wait
and there is something ominous
in the way they bend their back.
The moment is there in the first curve
the rock follows, the bald blackness
cut by storm and scored to sharp-
edged presence.

You learn folklore here
and magic. Legends from the shapes
of stone. Where the stream takes a bend
you sense a message shifting
on the stretch of sand where the fires
burned and the wind whirls
in a column of glass. Yesterday
a house gutted. Today already
kikuyu through the ashes.

At night you notice how close the stars
are / and how they seem to breathe.

This then is your four season window
through which fragmented scenes
make up their minds about detail
as though memory were signals
the sea picks up in its roaring
silence / and throws to the wind
under the door.

[1815] *'I'm carrying with me a heap of mountain*
ranges, tracks and creeks in my pocket.'

[1982] Also a cityscape.
The chart I have mapped
is by no means
finished.

CROSSINGS

Crossings

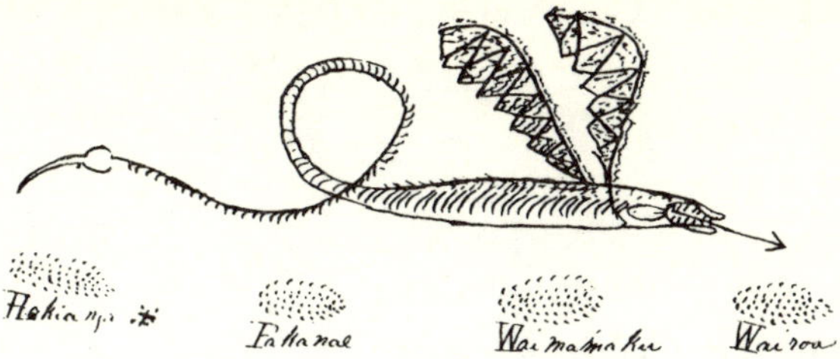

Above the North a taniwha flicks [Waimamaku]
its tongue towards Wairoa. Its tail loops
all the way back to the coast.
Its eye maps the always insistent horizon
brooding in timeless distance across
the consciousness of land. Flexed in flame
wings are sharp set sails
filled with the exultation of isolation.
Always beneath, that stretch of water and earth
marking the end and the beginning of all
stories, the narratives of exile explored as wingbeat
above tumultuous waves. Here history is close.
You hear it in the rhythms of wind roaming
where dark meets light and sea joins earth
in celebration of journeys, the pathos of space
where the heart lies.

Here I Give Thanks to Mondrian & McCahon &

[the migrants] We flew in like gannets at Muriwai [1951]
hovering on the currents of wind. [1939-45]
Sea was our element. Immediately
[Tasman Sea] on that coast, we were home.
In that wilderness rising we saw the light
translucent through dark and the ancestors
auspicious in stars to sight our way. Memory ['o yes, it can be
flashed through hills folded in secrets dark here and
but found the gap lifting the horizon manuka inspiring
beyond infinity. The landscape swept itself can breed despair.'
through sky McCahon]
into the fictions of love. In the distance
waves sing waiata, stories woven by water
and far away to seize the heart
and eye.

Discoveries

For Eendracht and Heemskerk in 1642
and Beth Serjeant in 1987

Poems for the future, you said, and ideas
exploded like supernovae shooting
in all directions, lighting up the page
and the signs drawn across just discovered
land *'Hoog en dor en zeer steil'* full of sand
corners to escape from with small details
charted in poems made with strange tongues;

'Goede reede en zeer effen water
op 25 Gr. 24 Min. Z. Br. voor Z. W.
en ooste winden, hebben de N. W. hoek
omtrent een kanon-schot in 't W van Zig,
op 10 vadem zand grond.'

                                        Something
happened. The details are not clear. Was it
the scenery grabbed them? Lines end quickly.
White spaces cross back across seas and ship-
wreck and landfall on unknown stretch of sand
sharper than glass cutting questions on stars
scattered a thousand years
gone.

Finding the Ancestors

Mangonui, Northland

It starts with paspalum and a grave
stone tucked away in high grass.
The wood has weathered and grows
colour in spreading lichen. The date
is an indentation three fingers wide.
The name's been wept out. It was hard
country and only the shape is there
rounded as hills or the church window
blank in all that blue glare of sky
just down the hill round the corner
in the lee of the tree that holds its own
stories. Only the freesias give something
away. A woman perhaps writing a tale
in the planting of bulbs. The tree nods
the wind whistles a tune you think
you've heard before, but across the bay
it's whipped all trace of landfall
away. There are few details.

Inheritors

To Amelia / 6 February 1980

'They made our mother grow old'

you said, reading the diary
where the old lady spun her web
of words fragile as dawn on dew
in a valley where all sound is a twist
of wind as it curls
up the beach; the moan of trees holding
the earth up despite failure and generations
dead
scanning the pace of silence.

Amelia, *'of loving, several ways.'*

These words you will know / will recognise
as days stretched beyond years
of remembering into history
we make
daily.

I see your mother in her garden also
the double cheerfulness that flowers
early, the smaller suns called daffodil.
Home a small place perched on a hill
looking out across islands. In winter
the polishing of gourds.

But unusual
winds began to blow from over the harbour
where storms raged and shouted like children
riding a brawl wave / baring white teeth.
Rips and currents breaching in all directions.

The tumult, like curls of weed, fumed
on the beach, made ragged stone
with too much bruising.

Bulbs were uplifted.
Journeys made
North.

Home then a small place curled in the lap
of the bay under the hill whose spine stood
straight in shafts of light at sunrise
protecting by distance and a sign saying:

leave your quarrels
in the waters of this river
as you enter the world of Taratara

also a peace flag flying:

leave your weapons
on the edge
as in Delphi weapons were

and everything sleep-eyed but wide awake
for the warm and cold side of the mountain
and the cleaned and scraped bones of ancestors
called back.

Was it McCahon who asked 'At the boundary
can I forbear from turning
my head?'

I rifle through histories and everywhere
people I recognise in you, landscapes,
and almost always, approaching clouds of pain.

On the flanks of Taratara
the ledger of ancestors sculpted
                    in trees
                        waterfalls
                        rivers
                        the songs the birds make
                                    when it rains
                        stones turned over
                                    to talk
                                        in the hand

and in everything   the calling
of names, the register of family
dispersed by whatever weather
to the corners of grief,
to come and give to the land
the korowai.

Bereavement

For Opa Dirk of Groningen, who died July, 1955

Mother, standing at the door
saw death across
the sea / whirling a snow of cloud.
Sun seared her eyes,
circled its mark there ten years too soon;
stretched white the bone,
pulled taut the line of the horizon,
tightened the distance grown cold in islands.

He was our first loss —
the family grew small / drew in upon itself.
We became   vulnerable
to the winter wind that blew from the north.

They buried him with little pomp.
In all that summer show of fragile light
no flowers marked his course.
We know he would have wanted them   and so
make roadside blossom here to match his way.

At our end of the world, world's end,
the garden wept winter.

Later there were cards / black-edged,
brought by a boy on a bicycle
riding the metal road gutted with rain.

Fires from Chagall

For my father

Shapes. Signatures of larger worlds
somersaulting out of the window
open to trees, the plain street
outside where the rain is caught on
an open umbrella, and a fiddler
dances in a night lit up from inside
listening houses while the sky burns
and everything
is ambiguous and quite changed from the last
time you looked.

In the line you draw   such notions
grow that we hear the hiss of the sun
as he kisses the water
goodnight / and what is
might go in any direction
of loss / where legends take root
and roads become symbols
of danger.

Past is place and shape.
A house in a street with a square
of grass where you might see
the sky falling between walls
standing like trees touching
each other with darkness.
But I say nothing of
childhood when everything is
clear   and lines belong
to burnt-ochre faces in portraits
that might smile
as if the moon had passed
through a shadow

and left
night tied up
in columns of death / notices
under the arm of the evening star.

I go in to bury my father.
He is not a man
I recognise other than
images I have seen
before / his eyes are closed.

The light has gone from the lamp.
Under the tree the talking
has vanished and singing
is motionless in clouds / looking
for skies that breed on all that
detail of frown and restless waves
you fared on / at the edge of winter
when salt lines drew naked wind
straight from the sea scarring
this shore.

Autumn should have been
as simple as a Cezanne fruit
garden, but you were miles away
across oceans, migrating.
The search always for the other
side of whatever it might have been
you were looking for.

Winter falls here in summer   this year.
In your birthplace record snow
storms are broadcast, intense
cold. Also appropriate.

Father, I should have touched you,
met whatever region of warmth was
in the colours you were before
the ice crept into the timid walls
of your room.

The picture is described.
The grey more sad than any pencil
mark can make on paper. Photographs
are left in drawers
but the image, I fear, will remain
a dream / far from
ending. Already
I see
the beginning.

A sequence of events signalling
danger / a network to decode
and songs for a death coming
suddenly clearly among sirens
wailing in a street full
of movement and light / shades
of bizarre mimes making
pastiches for writers to make
pieces of paper
to toss up to the sky like a flight
of so many coloured dragonflies
or the beautiful bird listening
to music starred with poems
serried as notes on a frail stave
of lines coming
together as tiny rainbows.

These pictures are the smell of a poem hung
up to dry like linen in the damp night
when sounds might break through the window
into that space where suddenly
a tear is the music stars make
in the calligraphy of trees.

The words speak for themselves
but the colour is personal / sombre
or black / depending on the gesture;
the way the earth might burn
orange or bitter as the lemon tree
very pretty and small in yellow
days when houses fall.

What matters is a sense of order;
the table under the stained-glass window,
the rattan blind down against sun,
the mat on the floor facing
Mecca where such colours might come
from rocks and sand blowing
through bleached grass and the tree
of life / firm
and reaching to the mihrab
where the holy city
lies.

Photographs

For my father

Strange how time works everything
into perspective. At *that* time
that age I wouldn't have thought
we had anything (much)
in common
and now, half way through
(and more if you believe that bit
about *three score years and ten*)
there you are in all three
generations going to school on the mantelpiece
taking the future
seriously.

In all three that same look
with just a curve of a smile
around the corner.
We're all between
five and maybe seven.
You could be
a little older. The two of us
have just heard the last shots
of childhood wars. [1914 - 18]
You are to hear mine again [1939 - 45]
later. James paints rainbows
and we walk through streets
with many others wanting
peace in our time.
We look a little as if
we'd seen something / (seriously)
around the corner.

Naming

The son is named after his mother's
father. Theo for short. Gift from God. His
sons carry the respective names of
grand and great-grandfathers. Men
are important.
Hendrik, Joseph,
Theodorus, Dirk.
One way of keeping close
to family we'll never see again
except in photographs. Two
for Calvin, one Catholic
and a communist who rolled ball bearings
down the street during union strikes. He lost
an eye on a wharf loading timber and didn't
smile much. Our son too bears the weight
of history. Generations of settlement
here and elsewhere across oceans / all leaving
their small stories on the postage stamp
landscape of our existence. All scattered
and gone / on journeys into pages
of mythology.
The younger branch opts for modernity.
They are not migrants.
They name their children after clowns, gods,
a Russian princess counting pence
in Woolworths after the revolution. Anything
not to hear those schmaltzy songs
expatriates might sing, hand over bleeding
heart in postures of melancholy. Everything
to avoid the pain of past / images of eyes
asking too many questions /arms raised
in wavering
farewells.

Labour Day — New Zealand

A holiday, and we plant tomatoes.
Traditional, you tell me, and there'll be rain
to see them off to a good start.
I think of red and flags and singing anthems
in the streets across oceans; shouts, blood [Groningen]
and a handful of ball bearings my grandpa carried
in his pocket for protection against hooves [police]
those days in May when everyone went marching.
It's a long time ago. Here we just burn spring fires,
sift soil for seed, sow beans for literature
and revolution. Nine rows. [Yeats]
At evening wind sets up, flares the fire
that's smouldered and with its sudden surge
we hear massed choirs and joyful feet.

Interior

In all the stories round the table
we were always going
back. The table too
did a lot of talking. It gave a lot
away. *Brood met kaas en worst,*
uitsmijters, biscuits met muis, koek
en Kerstkrans at Christmas tied with red
ribbons. After three tries
we gave up *oliebollen* on old year. Too
hot and all that blue haze
getting at the pictures. The smell
hung around for days and it wasn't the same
outside on the bar-b-q. You had to
have snow and *anijsmelk* and we weren't
in a Brueghel painting *'skating on the edge*
of a pond'. [Auden]
Flowers though were constant. Always
on the table a vase of sun
on the thick, rich tapestry hanging
quite like a seventeenth century 'still life
with *roemer*'. Even the plate [Willem Kalf]
reminds — blue-white porcelain
symbol of longevity. Cobalt of
purest sky and big
bowls of fruit de Heem would have treasured. [1606-1684]
Brass candlesticks aglow with polish,
a *'pronkjuweel'* under colonial verandah-
end windows in kauri, red-green
and timeless Vermeer yellow
but different entirely. A reality
Siddell might have painted, catching
and reflecting off objects in a room

not even half a lifetime old where everything
is straightbacked and upright. Solid
heart oak, well-travelled, diffused
with a warm light also
from the portraits on the wall smiling
a little sternly at their own
predicament. A view from Delft
in Dargaville. *'Vanitas vanitatum /*
ijdelheid der ijdelheden /
all is vanity.'

Fictions

All the past was what you remembered
and were told. Every street became [Groningen]
a memory, adventures you could walk in every day
from any paddock on the bottom of the world.
The map was in your heart, your head and all
the stories told by candlelight in cellars [1939-45]
waiting for planes to take their terror out. Everywhere
you met the old, the distant families and friends
in pictures reeling through dark afternoons
next Mrs Thurstons's milkbar in a Northland town.
You took to reading everything,
sang battle songs for wars 400 years ago.
You tricked the language into thinking it was now,
your eyes into seeing Van Streeck in your own table. [still life with
bowl, 1687]

Twelve thousand miles away you followed
your shadow through *linden* past *Schuitendiep*
and all the time be fishing eels
off butcher's wharf where the river churned
and ripped past the log carrying the taniwha upstream [Tangowahine]
to *'the place where the woman was taken'*.

You could walk for weeks and not get tired.
Small clouds of ash behind your heels in the far
interior of dreams. You knew the taste of wind
round the southeast corner through the rose
trellis of 't *Princenhof* where the sundial spoke
an ancient language you didn't believe. *'Tempus
Praeteritum Nihil'* [the past is nothing]. On another
century's clockface the sun went down and you could feel
a storm, run for shelter from the flying tiles
on old, old gables
in Mangawhare
where all the roofs were tin.

Schierbeek boven Howick

Voor Thea en de families

Nu zijn ze alle drie dood.
De vader, de moeder en Bert Schierbeek. Allen
op hun manier heengegaan
naar de lucht, de hemel, de sterren.

Ik zie ze elke avond. Stevig
arm in arm als schaatsers over 't Dampsterdiep naar 't Oosten.
Klaar, helder, fonkelend wit als ijs in een schilder's landschap.

Soms zweven ze even alleen
maar toch samen, gemoedelijk naast mekaar in de avond
als punten van de Driehoek, de sterren in de Phoenix
die vrede, schoonheid en kalmte brengen.
De rijkdommen van Zen
de streling van vlammen
die weer vorm geven. De lucht ruist
met namen, flakkert met herinneringen.

Ik herken ze als ouwe vrienden. Alle drie
lange verhalen man, en moar proat'n.
Zij schateren in het pronkjuweel van woorden.
Nemen het serieus. Kijk hoe aandachtig
ze elkaar verstaan. In de hoge
tempels van licht
zingen de dichters. Drie van 't Noorden
in de zuider nacht.

Als je luistert,
heur je grunings.

from
SPELLS FROM CHAGALL

Poems in celebration of
Helen Shaw, friend and poet

Blue Leaves Clapping

Helen, your blue leaves reached
me across pages
startled as frozen streams.
Among letters, words
many, your poem so fragile
surely
the ice would break
if one crossed.

It is evening. I am waiting now
for eight o'clock
listening to three minutes
before Amichai will come.

I wanted to say
I like the leaves
you wrote on the ice blue
delicate as light
paper / the line of birds
so distant in the always
present sky.

Here is the clapping / now
Amichai will tell sad stories / sing
death of friends.

As a child I remember
grandfather running.
It was spring. Flowers were shot
out of the sky hanging
red-breasted in parachute silk.
They fell and lay curled
in so many colours on the green
verge in the middle of the street,
torn and bunched up ancient as just
born children.

It is Friday. The silence
I had so much looked forward to
is simply an empty house.
The wood hurts in the fire.
It is exhausted.
All day it has whimpered.

Nails are driven on the hill
next door. Another house.
There are so many things
which will never
again be doors to worlds newer
than finding the first tree
to sit under / branches spreading
a net to catch stars
the sun scatters like rain
in the wind / blowing.

Helen, my words have gone
in another direction again. Your blue
leaves fallen among my broken trees
and tears in the sky
but know I read your dreaming
clouds
and marvel
at the clear
light.

House Woman Cloud

I *'Photograph'*

The light is on the paper and your hand
shapes the words dancing
'in the amphitheatre of the poem'.
The sun catches you / in white
the curtains hang on either side.
Fabric falls to billow
out (as cloud) with light
clouding in from the oriel
behind you. Your hair too
sweeps in this curving way
the poem makes on the page
in sunlight. You are already
spirited away through the lattice
window.

'14/6/85'

The early sun too hot
it's clouding
over / and later
the sky will answer.

Already light / thunder
in this winter burning
heat over the city.

III *'Concert'*

Sound mass and I take cover.
You would have liked these Rimmer *Clouds*
the fragile rain caught
in drumbowl and bells,
the curtain of brass moved by
a passing hand swaying the wind
and holding the shadows
spellbound.

I look to the clouds
some sign that death isn't
these scattered surfaces of dying
leaves in winter rain.

The sky breathes
a rush of wind.

'Purewa 17/6/85'

Any moment now the horizon
could slip away. Certainly
that tree looking through the window
trying not to be
noticed / could be
framed. Is still / stretched
out.
The setting is right /
also the frame (of mind).

Any fool can hang
a painting on a tree
but try

house woman cloud
cloud woman house

and all the lines between
making magic
myth of light in windows
cut / by branches.

The shadows stay
to light the way.

Later there was talk and very easy
the way the dark rolled
back from the day. The sun took
a breath of air / smiled
quietly from behind clouds where he'd been
thinking the trees looked a little thin
and lean / needed cheering.

Where the shadow falls / the light
talks, shivers
a little through branches.

There is no distance
between us
often / I dream
blue / tree / cloud
open
window.

Shadows on Glass

I
This death is the sunlight
caught in the branches of pohutukawa
beginning to swell at the buds
and bursting soon its firework
shooting red and sombre from this
midwinter twig swaying now
with cloud and shadow in light /
glass / scratching at flying skies
green worlds in blue.

The unexpected happens. The sky
bleeds. The lovers perform
no action. The stained glass is startled
light. Flowers blaze and their plumage
is a peacock's at the water's edge.

Dream landscapes might be
like this. Dark men taking memory
to themselves and speaking
in the multiplicity of silence.

II
Photographs are brown and large
grouping what ancestors could be caught
in the forever frame of features
you recognise quietly in children playing
under trees or wrapped in camellias
pale and gentle by the doorway.
You sit at night with their stories
long in the telling from other countries.
The lamp burns and lights the window
as if Rembrandt just walked by.
On the walls the shadows
rearrange themselves.

Trees are anchored
in the sky. Even the wind
doesn't move them.
We catch ourselves / out
trying to order memory / dream
the way / light
falls.

The changing mood and colour
of evening leaves us with our lives
walking along beside that body
we no longer recognise from the dream —
that spring, that bright green
so many years ago under an old oak
(pohutukawa, totara, beech — the detail
too darkened) an image
on the photo we didn't
take.

III
After all to be very quiet now
and let the tree speak
its special language remembering
words are shade
that will not answer
anything we ask.

Signal Blue

The poem as tea ceremony

This is the blue I've been looking for.
The court sits in a Persian manuscript
on mosque blue in the British Museum.
1397 colours an ancient tale.

Majnun in the desert.
Gouache on paper. Another blue. Later.
It is the blue of the night
sky you mistake for dawn / the blue
in the centre of the mihrab
or K'ang Hsi
sapphire in porcelain.

[azure
lapis lazuli
byzantine
manganese
ultramarine]

The stones in the garden are blue
where the shadow falls.
I make tea. Helen
you would have liked this ceremony,
the special room simple as bending
green bamboo caught forever
in medieval gardens *where everything
moved at a slow pace.*

'Focus attention on a few objects / of beauty.' [Sen'o Tanaka]

60: 'The ash in the brazier is moulded with a spoon.'
70: 'Wet ash is scattered on the pattern.'
76: 'The powdered tea is scooped up.'
77: 'Boiling water is ladled into the bowl.'
78: 'The tea and water is blended with a whisk.'

*Pick up the bowl in your right
hand and place it in the palm
of your left*

make a small bow
of reverence.

Brushstrokes for eternity / each
                                        a single movement.

I watch the antics of clouds
building in the buildings
all done with mirrors.

white / blue blue / white
the sky a simple cobalt.

from

THE 'K.M.' FILE AND OTHER POEMS WITH KATHERINE MANSFIELD

Composition

Dear Katherine, if this portrait does not
resemble, think of Picasso telling Gertrude
'it will'. Reality lies
in how you see things. For a short while
you give meaning to a teapot, the scuffed nose
of the sunday-take-him-out-of-the-box
fox, a sprig of blackberry, a tiny piece
of almond cake and the way grapes reflect
the colours of the carpet.
And then you vanish
from sight under a black silk shawl
alive with *'flowers fruits and birds'*
in a delicate handmade
garden.

Another Exile Paints a Spring Portrait of Katherine Mansfield

For Eric McCormick

There are all these lines
without words telling you a whole
story. The portrait is a yellow table
a gingko leaf shaped fan you think
might smell of sandalwood, a paperweight
some flying sheets of paper and a Chinese
vase of *'yellow-grey, 2 blues and brown'* [guess who]
curving itself round mountains and the wide open
branches of trees looking up river. Also an apple
halved, on a plate with knife and rose. Maybe
there's a cat asleep beside the blue cup. Certainly
a teapot (and you fill in the cake from the corner shop).
Everything is luminous and shines. Green
makes a slight impression on the wind
flowing in the way sky runs
through the open window snaring the light
on a jug of jonquils catching fire
at the edge of spring.

And there's your *still-life portrait* [yes, you've got it,
landscape in a figure. Frances Hodgkins]

Katherine Mansfield Contemplates a Painting of Elizabeth 1 (1533-1603)

For Roy Strong and Julia Trevelyan and their book

[*Journal*
Sept 1920]

'apples flashed like stars' in the orchard of your gown
running quicksilver riot with all the beasts
of paradise. Birds, worms and snails,
rainbows, flames and butterflies. Whole trees grew
in your wardrobe, bushes of mulberry, bright pomegranates,
mountains, swords and grasshoppers and everywhere strange
dark eyes guarding the *'hanginge sleeves embrodered*
with antiques of golde and silke of sonderie colours'.
Pineapple trees and oranges and all the seasons' flowers
flourished on your petticoats, figs almost
'broke in one's fingers and tasted of wine
and honey' yet in that blaze of passion everywhere
something I recognise in you; that startled
stare, those looped tears of pearls
heavy as muscat grapes, *'small glowing lamps of loss'*
pulsing minutely, a faint shadow of sadness
under the temple left of the eye and in the background
pluck of virginals.

[Item]

[*Journal*
1920]

[poem by
Elizabeth 1]

'... such change grew in my breast
that neither day nor night since that could I take any rest.'

Recipe for Rhubarb

From Katherine Mansfield

Two sticks of rhubarb depending
on the money and who's coming
to dinner. One local paper (out
of date will do), one gas stove.
Snip up the rhubarb and put in
a saucepan. Add a little
water and bring to the boil reading
the news or items
of interest. Virginia's written
a review. Turn the gas down
to a pinch and continue to savour
the full flavour of burning. Take off
the rhubarb and cool
also yourself with great goblets
of clear water flecked with gold-
fish.

Zen and the Art of Gurdjieff

It was cold at Fontainebleau
but the old peasant knew
a thing or two. Cows kept the place
warm and heat rises. You
had the best spot ['small and plain
and plenty of apples. At night and very simple']
you could watch stars and follow
one exit from the labyrinth [words & symbols]
trapping you. (*'Literature*
is not enough.') The idea
was to learn to laugh a little. Poke
fun and hear the sound of one hand
clapping. ['who am I']
When you looked again there was the face
before you were born. Simple
and necessary freedom. *'If you want*
the kernel break the shell.'
If you want nakedness take off
the coat *'and live in your body*
again' — the real 'real' — and be careful
of cold or you might catch
your death.

The K.M. Signature as Zen Painting

For Antony Alpers

No doubt about that fine down line turning
up the tail end of a winter
branch. Definitely
Niten's *Shrike* and maybe Tohaku
is there making mountains
in the morning mist. Fenollosa
might have had a hand in it
or Mu-chi (*'Kingfisher on a dry reed'*).
Quite simple the way valleys rise
and fall and slide black
and white with that brush of hand
on paper so quiet it is almost
a still life.

Love Affair

A given poem from Katherine Mansfield
with thanks to Helen McNeish

You wrote the table
was laid
for two
but nobody came
so you dined opposite
a white napkin.

It's called giving yourself
to life.
Through the window
a quiet branch
has the evening
to itself
also.

K.M. at Garsington

The flow of pen scratching
bars on paper / small prisons
to hold herself and the shade
of vision / the bright beams
of sun taking off
as so many
freedom doves clapping
delighted above lavender
& rosemary (that's for remembrance)
the pot-pourri
of gardens all
around
the blue scent
of life
fragile
on the open page.

Mansfield's Baths

Poem for the Katherine Mansfield Centennial Conference, *Wellington, 1988, with special thanks to Alan Thompson who wrote a letter to the* Listener *about Beethoven*

According to Schindler who knew
him, Beethoven was fanatic
about washing. Used to throw buckets
of water over himself in the bath.
Much of it went through the floorboards
and landladies got angry.
He had to change
house twenty-seven times. Imagine
the drain / on energy
and it made me think of Katherine
Mansfield. All those addresses.
She must have made a hundred
moves from one mansion to another
cottage, living her life out
in baths, maybe. One way
of keeping warm in England.
[letter to Anne Estelle Rice] Why else call her lung a *'water-wing'*
as though to float on,
[letter to J.M.M. 22 Dec 1917] and write *'the world is only water*
that flows ...'. What better place
'close to the wall' to *'make up*
a little basket of dreams', move about
and exercise gently, the water
[letter to J.M.M. 13 Dec 1915] waving *'like a school of fishes'*
over the edge.

I am reading through all the *Lives*
and *Letters* checking for *'buckets'*,
'landladies', *'baths'* and *'rotten floorboards'*.
There may be a thesis in it.

Last Portrait

There are no smiles
in this photo. You look straight
into the lens / the unblinking
eye of death
staring you in the face. The mouth
gives a lot / away. Too cherry red
for picking in the intense cold
as though the Arctic had swept
over Fontainebleau and spilt blood
from the wind tearing *'nor'north* [letter]
by east nor'east'. If you know
a colder one it is there
in that small image so frozen
you could skate over it.

WHAT SHALL WE TELL LI PO:
POEMS FOR CHINA

Inner Gardens

For Zhang Weiping in prison

I
Nine years is a long time
to keep darkness company
but remember the story of Lan
Xiang Cheng. A wise man. He fell
in love with landscapes and seasons. Spring
was his favourite. All that blossom
and promise. It lasts
only a short while. The wind comes
and the rain and it's gone. He wanted
to hold on to spring. Keep it about
himself a little longer. So he built a study
in his garden in the mountain and called it
'study containing spring'. That way he kept youth
with him for a very long time.

II
You are in Hangzhou where green is predominant
and shadows are luminous with mystery
along the banks of Sai Wu. Each scene cut [West Lake]
perfect as if through window frames. Paths
of sunlight cutting across the silhouettes
linking where you stand with a distant
view. Here too the bridge with the seven
pavilions. The roofs like birds taking off
on outstretched wings / gentle brushstrokes
flashed in orange and copper sulphate.
You may not have a window / some small space
to look out and keep in touch with willows
bending with the wind for centuries, and everything
is for a very long time but try to be
like that mother of the emperor who changed [Qian Long]

the summer palace in Beijing. She took her favourite
landscapes with her in her mind and planted them
wherever she was forced to live. That way she was
always surrounded by tranquility / the blue hazed hills
and quiet reflecting water
of longevity and peace.

III
T'ai-Chi Ch'uan

If the space where they keep you
the next years is just a little
larger than the length of your outstretched
arms, you will be able to visualize clouds
and move them away with a slow, graceful turn
of your hand should they frown
or darken to form rain. A few movements
will shape you trees to shade your head
and the hard board of your bed
will be earth soft in late spring sprung
bright with flowers and new grass. You
might be tempted to tense a melon
out of the early vapours of air and imagine
oh, imagine that cool caress for breakfast.
These small acts will make you
strong, subtle as ink
handscrolled on paper all those centuries ago. [Li K'an]
Remember the story
told of the woman in prison.
She knew Beethoven well. From inside
each day she conducted a quartet. Each part
separately in her head then putting all four
instruments together silently as she sat there
in solitary confinement. It took years
but the music lifted the sky
into that darkness and the sun
gave back her life.

The Hundred Flowers

The old men kept gardens.
They liked order and tidiness.
Small clusters of colour. Mostly
red. Each year they would sow
seeds for a hundred flowers
to blossom and bring smiles
to their old faces. Always
the flowers would bloom
briefly, the old men laugh
at their brightness and the way
they seemed to breathe together
in unison, opening out their petals
to the sun. Each year too
the laughter changed as suddenly
to rasping wind, a squall, a catch
of fire from the dragon's whim
and the hundred flowers withered
before they had smiled
one day.

What Shall We Tell Li Po

Tiananmen Square, June, 1989

What shall we tell Li Po [701 - 762]
now that dragons claw at skies
and the sun's a goblet of blood.
Somewhere a lute turns into wood
and trees change pale as jade.
What shall we tell Li Po
now that wind breathes fire
into the summer square and iron
horses plough the streets.
What shall we tell Li Po
now that the young are swept
as autumn leaves for burning
and the smell of death
is incense in the streets.
What shall we tell Li Po
now the new moon's caught
in ragged branch of ancient trees
and the cinnabar sky flies
a torn black flag.

KIRIKAU

For William (Bill) Trussell

Kirikau (the place where a battle was fought by men stripped naked) is a small settlement about twenty miles down the Wanganui river from Taumarunui. The large isolated area around it was offered for sale to soldiers returning from the First World War.

Late in 1989 we made a pilgrimage back to the place where some of the family had spent their summer holidays as children, helping on the 'farms' wrested from the forests. These poems are a response to the journey.

Tawata (I) — Beginnings

After every war it happens, you say.
Poor buggers. First fight their guts out
on some piece of land in France
or Africa, some godforsaken hole
in Greece or wherever the soil is
rank with killing, then get them home
to a heroes' welcome, fanfares in streets,
and a bit of wilderness to break
in somewhere in the back blocks.
On their wedding day he was given two horses.
(One was called Dick. That much
is remembered.) Afterwards the two of them
set off, each guiding a packhorse also. It took four
days impatient riding to get halfway. Between them
they carried bags of flour, others
of salt, an axe, a shotgun and a 303 for pigs
and food. Matches too presumably.
They did a lot of burning. Neither of them bothered
much about landscape. Never spoke of grandeur. Wouldn't
have noticed the rata out in her best red at Christmas.
They were anxious
to get on. A tree was only worth the hard wood.
What was the point of sitting under shade watching
the leaves change colour when the sun chatted up the birds.
They knew their proverbs and laboured. Their first
children were born under tarpaulin.
Later they were lent an ancient house on the bottom
flat next the river where the water roared over stones.

It lived at night
when they went eeling, with naked ghosts
of other wars talking from under the tawa trees.
Much later a leper lived there. When he died a neighbour
buried him. Also rough as the country he tried
to fence. Made the coffin too small. Chopped
off the legs to get him in. He was also a veteran
of that First War. Lost five sons
in the next one. Sometimes he thinks he hears the young
ones calling to him from below in the river and he stumbles
across the flat to watch them shooting
down the current in an old canoe, but always
it is only the splashing water and the moon
on the river stones lighting up a legend
white with bones.

Two different spellings exist for this place-name. While Tawhata is sometimes used, I have kept the one said to come from the legend surrounding Hinewaha who used to beat the tawa in that area to obtain fruit.

Bert

He was the second son. At twenty-five
he'd lived more than a life. Three years
in Egypt, Paschendale and right through
to Verdun and Ypres. Wipers
the boys called it and many were.
His oldest brother also. The sun
of his mother's eye. She never laughed
again. Her mouth hooked
hard as the kettle over the range
in the kitchen where she darkened her days.
For a while he bore corpses and the blown
up bits of friends on stretchers
across battlegounds. He never was the same
again. Couldn't sit still for a minute. No time
for comfort and 'idle chatter' he used to call it.
Even his chair was straightbacked and hard.
When morale was down he was one of the boys
in the band trading cannonshot for timpani. Another
kind of thunder he later made his living
in the silent movies. When it was over
he baked 200 pancakes with what small supplies
were left for the troops and drank one glass
of beer. Life was too precious and he was always
frugal. His one indulgence
a goose he walked on Sunday mornings
in a suit and never ate. Mostly he wanted
to make up the lost years and drove
at terrifying speeds. The point was to set your goal
and get there fast. He made it
past ninety.

Reg

There are different versions
of what happened. In one story
they didn't tell you how he had the bastard
rammed up in the race. Its horns caught
in the space between the 8 x 2's. Took an axe
and chopped them off. Better than mending
the rails and couldn't be bothered
to traipse all the way back home
for tools. Besides they expected him
for tea, to pass the cakes round
for the ladies. He had a charming style.
On Saturdays he dressed in white
for cricket. Sometimes he boiled
live eels in cauldrons on the range. They splashed
and screamed, but what the hell, he'd heard
it all before at Paschendale.
When his best dog took to worrying
a sheep he bashed its head in with a fence
post. No point
in having feelings. A man might die
that way. Sometimes at night
he thought the clouds frowned, the river
talked, but he knew it was only water
over the stones where the moon caught
the ripple of rapids laughing
round the bend. Next morning he would blast
the course and build a wall to change
the current, still the voices.

Lucy

The more they cleared the rougher it showed up
but she was young and strong and wanting
a world. She planted rhododendron
on slashed and burned ground, bleached bags
for sheets and shirts, held competitions
for who could make the best pyjamas, the nicest frocks,
guarding her floral scraps for trimmings.
The smaller bags made pillowslips and pinnies.
She was farming people and patched each one
with flowers in the centre. Sewed tea-towels
and mended broken chairs.
The nearest neighbour was two miles away
but it might have been another country,
it took so long to walk. The track kept slipping
down the bluff. Now there are signs
telling you not to loiter
and small malicious rocks hurl down abuse
in fretful clouds of dust.
The road is new and treacherous. The old one runs
above. Among the tufts of grass
the track is still discernible. That's where
they took a tumble in the night.
They could hear the band play in the Hall
and knew they wouldn't make it then, for supper.
Two horses killed
the buggy broken up. Arthur breaking
an arm. What happened to the woman
is not recorded. We know
she lived.

Molly

After Molly killed the man she became
a quiet chapter in their histories. No-one
talked of her again in front of children.
She was not pointed to in photographs
and everything about her lies
in semi-darkness, almost impossible to read.
We know Aunt Molly killed a man. That much
was told us. There were no letters. We never found
a diary filled with blanks to let you know how hard
the days, how little time was left for writing
it all down. In what images are left
the other family women look away.
You can not catch their eyes. They seem preoccupied
with what is happening in the hills,
the shapeful curves cutting the cerulean
sky. It got cold up there in the tin hut. The iron
chimney almost bigger than the house. An eight foot fire
at least was never out. The axe stood always ready
by the door. The draught whispered through the floor.
One imagines
she wore floral print and had her hair tied back.
She was a widow (*'such a big man too to die
of cold'*) and kept the farm
going. The gun in the kitchen always loaded.
The kids all did their share but how
she must have ached with all that
persevering. Each day began at dawn and finished
well into the night and now the house is derelict,
staring suspiciously through hostile growths
of scrub and gorse. Even the trees
seem thin and uninviting and you decide not to go
up the rutted hilly track. The wind whistles as a child
might when he's learning, and the branches catch
the eerie breath and pass it round with rustling hands.

Only the night strides here
with confidence. Almost immediately it's dark.

Maybe it was midday when he came. Maybe later.
The dogs would have barked.
She would have answered his knock on the door,
and offered food. The tea would have been on the boil.
She might have made a batch of scones and had him sit
by the fire to dry. The nearest farm was miles away.
She was at the end of the road, where her world
began. Perhaps they talked. He might have
fiddled with the silver sugar basin. She was thirty-five
and alone in the kitchen. Maybe it went to his head.
He must have suddenly gone for the axe by the door.
She reached for the gun that was always loaded
and blew his head off. You imagine
you hear dogs bark but it is only birds
disturbed against the fleeing sky
suddenly dressed in mourning black.

Kirikau — Endings

Much later they built a proper house.
Everyone came in *Hatrick's* from town to help.
It took the whole summer. Each day
the kids would swim, letting the current rush them
down past Tawa holding out her gifts
for Tutangatakina sleeping under Taniwha Rock.
That's how Sam died, they reckoned. Must have
caught pneumonia in all that heat. Only thirty
and a big man at that. Should have known
how the water was always too cold and disapproving,
the ice sharp teeth sinking right to your bones.
At night it spooked with stories
and sometimes you heard the trees laughing together
but all you saw was stars.
Sometimes they found an ancient tool of war
and hung it on the mantle with the gun. They shot
down rapids in a dug-out log
shouting to dispel their fright. At Christmas
there was a ritual. One dozen beer and twice
the lemonade for shandies. The empties carried
back to town, signalling the end
of summer. On Sundays they tidied up
the flower beds and planted gardens. The ash from the burns
made the onions grow. Also spuds and fruit.
Apples, plums and pears. Apricots perhaps
(the stories differ and nobody wrote them down)
walnuts from the fellow further down who lost
his acres to the *Loan & Mercantile.*
When the old man died they ran a chain saw through
the orchard. Ripped the buggers out. Now sheep graze
still and down the road wild apples
bloom.

Kirikau Haiku

Above the river
morning fog
drifts through

							s
							u
							p
p		**a**					p
o		s			**o**		l
p	**h**	t	**n**		l	**m**	e
l	i	e	g	**t**	i	a	j
a	n	l	a	a	v	h	a
r	a	i	i	w	e	o	c
s	u	a	o	a	s	e	k

Tawata (II)

Here maps fail you and history confuses. Also
the manner it records. Mostly you listen to stories
told from under trees, the way a stone talks
in your hand. Sometimes you can see how
the wind lies from a twisted branch. The willows
say the missionary felt homesick with his darkness
struggling up the river. Imagined himself back
'gently down the stream'. Maybe he wanted light
relief in seasons, autumn spectaculars in all that
grim foreboding, the messages he brought. Also Tawa
is sombre, the books tell you now there's not much
left but stumps that *'sit upon the ground and tell
sad tales'.* Other legends speak of beatings
and a woman picking fruit. Scars
are visible, also in those early pictures.
What possessed them you wonder to spend
their days slashing their way to the sky.
When the light fell all they could see was black
and columns of smoke rising. For a moment
the men might have thought
they were back at Paschendale but they were not
given to fancy, kept their heads down and went on
fighting. Sometimes they'd scratch an entry in a diary,
take a picture. Mostly the smiling is just round the corner
and you can't imagine why they dressed in collars,
enjoyed picnics on the charred persistent trunks rising
like Goya *Disasters* from the torn ground. Zadkine
is there holding up his hands in horror, where Edith smiles
'sitting on a rimu stump' the height of a man in her best
clothes. Even now the captions in their albums lie
their way from one book to another: *'The raw slips
in the hills behind were caused by rain.'*

Bill

Pehimahaka

This is where the road ends and your journey
begins again in the going back. You tell us stories
and the fires sweep through this first burn.
It is summer and the heat unbearable. We try
to keep to whatever shade has grown again
through the years you were in other landscapes,
and watch the smoke curling into the hearts of family
and hardening the small arteries of love. We see
their eyes narrow and mouths pull grim. Their shoulders
sharp chiselled against the felled spaces they emptied.
At night a million tears fall from the fleeing sky.
We ask questions and you answer. Your face does
not give away many directions. You keep the map close
to the past as if the pointing is painful and you are afraid
an icy wind will suddenly bluster across these bare summer
records of loss. A kereru knells a bell for the past
and our eyes follow a fence line you helped tighten.
You were eight, maybe younger. You carried the hammers.
Even the horse could hardly make it up that steep incline
and stumbled over torn ground stretching up forever.
You thought the peak reached into heaven. It took days
lugging everything up. The rolls of wire clawed the flesh,
ripped open clothes. The posts seemed heavier than crosses
at Golgotha. You learned your first lessons here in hardness
and as you tell the story we watch the hammer somer-
saulting all the way down to where we are in the bottom
of the gulley and a small boy falling to fetch it and starting
the long climb back. Sheep are white flecks
against that barren hill where your fence now struggles
to keep upright. It has weathered sixty years. Lichen gnaws
at its bones and its skeletal frame is twisted.

I look at your hands and see fine lines net
together the fragile web of past, threading in and out
through lives watching from shadows.
At night we cook the pehu found growing wild
on the river flat. Our small circle of stones a ritual
fire. The hills crouch and tense darkly. They too
are remembering stories crackling with past
where the sun overturned and blazed through nights
shrilling in a panic of birds fleeing
the vanishing sky. They eye the glowing
tongues suspiciously, anxious to see the Upoko-
roa children won't suddenly leap out and break
into that devastating language echoing
still from their ochre slurring scars.

from
DEAR MR SARGESON ...

lighthouse

For Dennis McEldowney

Poetry is the only thing
you can rely on, you said
increasingly as you grew
old. The only life worth
bothering as you kept now
out of the light
inside the hedge. Fewer tomatoes
less peppers more underlinings
to texts other than your own.
Milton for solace and a sense
of deliverance, feeling perhaps
not quite to be lost in a world
going to hell and everyone *just*
trespassing thanks. You'd had *more*
than enough. A time for sowing
over and reading now at first light
in winter / needing
bare branches. At Shoal Bay
even the water doesn't come up
anymore and only the house
stands for a while grey
as a weathership in heavy
swells coming off the road.

life

On your shelves few strangers
have been taken in. Some Greeks
yes and a Frenchman also
familiar. Otherwise your friends
are English and American. Local
of course. Maurice and Maurice
and Maurice and Karl. Janet is there
intensely as *owls do cry* incandescent
at the edge of the alphabet. But mostly
you liked chaps. Buddha and Krishna
conspicuously absent. Zen also
and persimmons in a bamboo hat.
A practical room
startling as a still life
without chrysanthemums.

writing

For Craig Wallace

I do not see Rumi
on your shelves. You'd have liked
him. The beginning
of singing. Poems reaching up
along your beach. Branch and tree
all the words skating in
'roots and all'. Hokusai
on a surfboard. The driftwood
you gathered for winter
fires.

detail

If I lived here I would scrub
this bench to burnishing, oil it
chestnut red for warmth and ask
the lotus-holding Buddha to sit next
a bowl flame orange with persimmons
stroked in sun. The traffic noise outside
would be the sound of flowing water.
Hear the wind rising,
the waves far off,
turning over.

poetry in the afternoon as it might have been

Look at all the words
on the table. Quick
grab them. Pink yellow
brown green blue the vase
in the sun full of flowers
catch them on paper
arrange them as you might
knife fork plate with fruit.
Later you can change it
to prose. Tougher
on the heart. Leave out
the colour but add red and the sky
falling upward
among gooseberries.

salon with a difference

For Una Platts

The eighteenth century wouldn't have
thought your bach would stand up
to all that clamour. Look at them all
on the wall. The local *literati.* No
money, no swank and everyone
on the margin. Only tea and beer
or *zwieback* and *Lemora.* Nothing
luxurious. No ornaments or dress
and mostly noisy. (*'Un peu de silence
s'il vous plait.'*) The talk jumping
from Plato to Proust. Everyone crowding
in remembering things past. Books
opened like veins in the blood spilling
the Duchess of Guermantes leaning out
the window to pick your peppers. Such
abundance and all that
douceur de vivre, yes?

simple

For George Haydn

To turn your bach
into a teahouse. *'Original-
ly there is nothing / but
the tea is good and finest
green.'* All we need is
George Haydn,
a sliding door and white
translucent paper. The ceiling
could be sanded down. Bare
texture is valued, also simplicity
and *wabi* — the sobriety
a puritan might enjoy if only
briefly. Harmony is everything
and quiet deliberation. Your spirit
already there stepping the stones
on the narrow path to all that
reflection.

a prose poem in the new age

After listening to an Austrian psychologist on the radio

'I vaz vanting to re-kreate dead people. All
ze time I vaz tinking vhat vaz ze funktion
of life? I uze ze komputer to simulate.
I started viz myself. Der vaz no problem.
First ze skeleton. 3D for ze outside look.
I give shape to ze komputer. A data-bank
viz body parts. Now
I kan make modifikations and lokal deformations.
The only trouble she like ze Barbie doll. Plastik.
Able to go zrou rooms, zrou doors
and show emotions. But difficult to get 100%
person. She talk, she smile, she make tears.
Ve are just at ze iceberg. Tomorrow maybe
I hav ze man.' (If you're in heaven, Sargeson
please ask God 'Help!') *'I vould like someone*
alvays available 24 hours. Ve vill improve.
Many people are lonely. Ve vill viz television be
in ze future. Syntetik actors for friends.' (You
too could be back at the squeeze of a mouse,
Frank.) *'Zen vill be happy times.'*

a story for you

From Judith Haswell

'A friend of a friend of a friend knew
I wanted to meet the writer so
he arranged an invitation. Strictly
by appointment. Half an hour
on Sunday. "Come at three." I walked
through the hole in the hedge
and proffered one small palmful of *ginseng*
(not wanting to make mountains).
He poured *Lemora* wine and sang
Beethoven's Ninth. For a brief while
we were *"Bruder"*, then the wind waved
and the air took wing across the waves
to Rangitoto.'

now

For Judith Haswell

In the shade of your great loquat
small seedlings reaching
for a splash of sun.

TALKING PICTURES

Building in Mirror Glass

Think of journeys / disconnected
pictures in the mind. Nothing
to do with reality. Flash of dark
glass in reflections. Your own floating
beside you, excited as wind
cutting corners on sharp streets opening
into fragments of blue sky you can touch
in all directions on these shining
surfaces you walk.

A Change in the Weather

For Lauris Edmond

Last night the sky turned red. It seemed
to bleed. The wind got up and a storm blew
itself through the surf breaking on the beach.
Trees keened and clamoured in *angst.*
I thought of earthquakes, some terrible destruction,
a national calamity, and turned on the teletext.
It read you'd died just then. For a moment
everything seemed very still
then tempest raged again. All night
I worried on mortality, but drifted
off to wake to rain and clouds in mourning.
Further south, floods are closing roads.
A deepening depression is expected
across the country.

Ladders

'like I have seen the dark green ladder climbing'

Baxter dreamt ladders
above rivers broken
in a might of force.
They were left hanging
vertiginous
ruins lamenting the wild one
in him. I lie awake listening
to the stillness rolling forever
in the sonnets of love and the moon
in the dark sky of soul.

A Whale in Auckland

For Jan Kemp, who stuck hers on the billboard

When you've written your poem
naturally you want to see it / riding there / right
with the whale on Queen Street
where he blows in the sun
sharp on the blue wall stretching
maybe 50 feet of protest.

A whole universe on a railing.
For simple people the limits of the world
floating where the news is made
and shouted daily on the corner.

An ancient spirit, sole survivor
of all those dead by Ahabs' spears
slashing for continents of loot
in the plentiful cathedrals
sounding their grave music
with the seawaves sweet
as ambergris.

A whale of a deity drifting there
where Maui might have fished before
the light got crowded out
by steel and glass competing for the sky.

An island, psalm leviathan as gentle
focus in a busy street / stretched far beyond
a local history marked on a paling wall —
the scaffold of crude time
when seas were torn with flinching flesh
slapping circles of blood.

See how his eye is turned back
as if some vague disquiet stirred
anxious at centres of water boiling
in outrage among headlands
exploding
in splay of shot and iron / ripped open
gashed
by grabs clawing marks on maps
charted perhaps an hour ago.

He has no need to fear.
Your poem right there / on the narrow horizon /
stuck in the belly of the whale.
A tiny Jonah casting misfortune's spell
on all who would deny this lord
the reign in Neptune's realm.

Dinner in the Creeley Mode

After reading bits about supper and things in Mate 25

I wanted to write a poem about fall
-ing leaves / Alfred Street with trees
roof high and higher / the sun
in the low afternoon streaking
through branches,
the ground heaped with brown
and the child leaping / running
scuffing the colours and sending
them whirling up and down again.

But Creeley waylaid me.

I wrote an itinerary once.
A poem about objects
cased as forever behind glass
in a mottled kauri cabinet.
Nobody wanted it.

So for luck I invited some guests:
four men and three women.
I arranged a table with food
a kauri table grained
with successive generations carving
their names and signs
(black stains on light wood)

I placed these chairs 

all curls and whirlygigs
creaking at the joints
with care around
prepared a menu to delight:

olives
red cabbage spiked with caraway / dashed with garlic
the hearts of artichoke
and aubergine with lemon sprinkled with parsley
nuts and rice and all things nice
wrapped in vine leaves
paté, calamaré,
every kind of entreé
a magnificent fish on a porcelain dish
(blue glaze on white stone (ware))
ringed all about with onion rings and spicy things

and bread and the plates scattered with sesame

and wine
and cheese
with names to relish
                    roquefort gruyere gorgonzola camembert
(nine pages in Larousse on the naming of cheese —
savour that).

I got tired of the dinner
the people
and looked out the window
but it was night and dark
and I alone in the glass.

Muriwai

Wind brushed, water washed
the sand grained with signatures
where gulls temporary as moments
flick their feet back into the sky
waiting for gusts.

Shadows now glide above us
and round the rock darkness stirs.
We walk and talk, picking up objects
we link with the past, exploring
the fragility of permanence:

the stories of lives in a piece of flotsam,
a gannet's quill to write midwinter rain
finer than drift stroking the curve of the coast,
sharper than whales etched on the horizon
in nineteenth century views.

Spirits wail and make in the sand
a watermark. At the sea's edge
gods breathe the lifted wave into song.

Hokianga Love Song

In the hollowed trunk of the puriri tree
wild bees have made honey. They hum
songs in the vault of shining leaves and drink
from flowers sensuous in the green dark.
We too have had our fill of nectar and watch
light crochet moving patterns of shade
through branches making wide verandahs. We lie
remembering how houses grew from local timbers
(kauri mostly, *Agathis australis,* with totara
for blocks) and the wind blew from up harbour
light as your encircling arms in this summer grass
tousled blond by sun licking its warm tongue
across our bodies salt with the sea where the taniwha
lives behind rocks wreathed in swirls of kelp. We
follow the tumbling drift of curves coming and going
and coming together again as lovers on tides undisturbed
by gulls, and in that turbulence our bodies are solemn
as hills that shape with the burden of stories older
than ancient weeping waiata and the naming of past
under the light blue winking leaves of sky.

Daffodil

For James

This flower is the sun, said the child
in the garden kicking alive
on the first day of spring.

Let us bring the sun into the house /
the sunburst day on fire
in the fray-torn circle of flame.

And so we cut it.
Persephone's pale lily gentle as wind
sighing in cathedrals of its heart.

Spring now bursts open on our household day.
The sun stands in a core of glow /
fountain of fire / to bear delight
as single stars bright
in the marble sky where light barely moves.

Blood Falls

For Nigel Brown

The walls of your room are swept
with ice. White seas rise
violently. Ancient winds catch the snow
sharper than pain.

You journey in drifts of light
exploring the textures of white
cutting a new calligraphy of silence
stretching always towards that immortal
line on the horizon.

You build cairns here to pin existence
that infinite fragility
we feel in our bones these moments
of endurance. Blood is drawn
from extremities. Paints itself
in iron oxide stains
on the flanks of distant hills.

Poems marking the bruise of life.

The Painter in Antarctica

For Nigel Brown

You watch the light taking its time
in the sky. A petrel skimming
the waterline, and all the colours of the world
momently white

and dark.

A whole new planet, hunched
and carapaced, making opaque all
memory in this clarity of ribs
sculpting the water. Here *'the tear
of things'* has only just reached [Wallace Stevens]
but deep in the pockets of horizons
streaks of crimson mark the heart.
Your charcoal captures the edge of white
in tomorrow's blizzard. Footsteps
for a while, then wind
runs the world alone.

Summer

For the painter returned from Antarctica

Talking about ice
I feel the sun in my bones —
voluptuous delight.

For Izumi

I
There are certain
constants you say, watching
the sea curl in Hokusai strokes
a poet might draw with portable brush
and ink kit — *'yatata'* you instruct
forming first words down a path
filled with shadows. The beach sighs
with all the journeys on paper
Basho wrote in the wind
that now weaves a scarf of incense
through your hair. Pine trees
and clouds stand still and envy
the way smoke brushes you
small poems.

Katsushika Hokusai: 1760-1849. Probably the best known and most loved of the Ukiyo-e masters. Matsuo Basho: 1644-1694. Haiku poet probably best known for his work 'The Narrow Road to the Deep North and other sketches'.

II

In this picture you take
the classical pose. A face
Utamaro would have caught
in one bold line. Flattering
the nape of the neck. A poem
writing the moon in snow on the mirror.
Your parasol a circle of red
roses in the sombre cedar garden.
Bushes are trimmed and small
stone lanterns throw shadows
on the golden darts of happiness
under the bridge with ten views.
From your face the sun is out
and you're wearing the same colour.
Even the trees are silent
watching you
take their breath away.

Utamaro: 1764-1806. Ukiyo-e master / printmaker especially renowned for his exquisite portaits of women. The poem makes indirect reference to his work 'Powdering the Neck'.

III

This photo shows you inside
the house learning the tea ceremony.
One of four accomplishments
Toyohiro might have cut, so quiet the hands
cupped round the four seasons
bowl you comment on and pass
for me to taste. Even the door
is in the right place, bringing in
the landscape and the women
arranging hydrangeas in angles
to catch the sun and all possible
shadows.
You are at home here with the other
details in your Saturday
life. Later you will pick flowers
for the alcove. Small treasure
to pleasure the scroll. Some day
you may take up brush
painting and poetry. Then we will write
waka and draw lines
lighter than winter cranes
stalking pines trees in thin white wash.

Utagawa Toyohiro: 1763-1828. A woodcut artist. Noted for a series of prints entitled 'The Four Accomplishments' showing Yoshiwara women engaged in daily activities.

Parables with a Four-Coloured Bowl, and for Yoshiko, Happiness

You offer rice, sharing the bowl
'with many colours in time of war'
when there was only sometimes
the bowl blue as stretched sky.

White grains. Simple
but fertile with symbols
speaking the language of mystics.
In the raked rhythms of life
we search for wholeness,
a reconciliation
fashioned in earth.

Red plums for youth, the blossom
forever in memory, the sun always
rising even in winter. That inner light
steadfast as words in the beginning.

Saffron spice and pickles. Our lives
the brush painting our portrait
on ancient scrolls. Every night
a new moon. Gusts of wind
translating the infinite into reverence.
On the rim of the world
our grateful ringing of bells.

In Camera

For Frank Hofmann – photographer 1916-1989

I
In all the pictures stacked up
along the walls of your house
there's none of you
recording the light, waiting
to *'fix the shadow'.* Plenty
of landscapes with wind through
rye-grass, hills folded against
an encircling curve of sky gearing up
for a fight with thunder and that split instant
chiaroscuro lightning
you were drawn to. Old-fashioned a bit
in your way. Quixotic as journeys
you captured in images
informing drawers and albums,
the pages of dated magazines. Footnotes now
in catalogues of exhibitions. Here
in the house you have departed, old histories
beside your own. Roman steps, gondolas
in ancient colours that might have been
autobiographical, some childhood
shots in Prague, a close-up
of a doorhandle that survived
the suffering where no-one inside did.
Your family, taking their place with
all these other portraits — famous
women, houses making records in other houses,
painters and all the notes of music massing
mythology here in a room facing the wrong way
and cold this winter
where everything seems to wait.

II

You tell stories to keep you
away from winter and the dead [Czechoslovakia
colour of white. On the wall 1939]
faces in sepia turn their heads to listen.
They are the ancestors from another
country living here in a different time
entirely, at home in your room
with large windows watching
the magnolia offer its cream chalices
in tribute to blues, the exodus green [Chagall]
spread candelabrum wide across
your narratives of exile. You conjure
memories from photographs. One
in particular catches your breath.
A door wrought with your family name.
All that is left
you say, and tell that story
and six million others. Turning
you are gaunt as a Giacometti
sculpture and leave your sentence
unfinished. 'As they say in Vienna ....'
Your hand touches a bronze hand
cast from a knee of a Buddha in Bangkok.
You couldn't afford the whole god
you tell me, 'but this is better by far
and without all that smiling.'

III

April 13, 1990

This year your death falls on black
Friday and in your other country
the churches would be draped
for mourning. Here we prepare for other
ways of making sense of dark
and light, your favourite style
in catching balance, a matter of fate
you thought, of resigning yourself
to taking a tower view.
Tonight you would have recognised
the Martinu played by your countrymen. Dark [String Quartet No. 5, 1938]
as the year you fled, scrawled over
with messages of loss. Handwritten notes
drawing lowest strings on melancholy, plucking
plaintive song from restless skies
and trembling through a passionate disquiet
into that tragic climax. All that suffering
your friend tells me, thinking of you, and I
see you hunch in readiness for Smetana. [String Quartet in E minor]
Fate rings a note again and insists you take
your life elsewhere, out
from the larger cities of the world to this
small plot.

Frank Hofmann was born in Prague and fled to New Zealand just before Hitler invaded Czechoslovakia. He worked here as a professional photographer. A major exhibition entitled 'Object & Style' — photographs from four decades — toured the country shortly after his death.

Advice from a Photographer

For Robert Cross

Your letter is a poem. What can I say
you say to unlock the Cartier Bresson
in you. Buy yourself a camera. But don't worry
about fancy electronic jobs. They'd remind
of Singapore where drains open
into streets hanging under silk
bright colours and greetings dance in
bunches of bananas under paper lanterns
the red-gold canvas sunscreens
sagging from colonial pillars. Drowsy
taste of spices tumbling on the awesome heat;
sounds of knives sharpening / screams
and a small cloud of down.
You can do it with two lenses. The 135
flattens perspective and heightens
whatever is going on and the 50 gives
an open feel, wide as a slashed neck.
Look for light and keep the pictures
simple. Remember you're starting
with reality but you don't want to finish
that way. It's only a photo,
a scrawny chook red on a piece of paper.
It can't answer back.

For Leon van den Eijkel

I 'The Artist in His Studio'

This, the man at the computer will tell you,
is satire. The poet no longer
pushes a pen. He's into the post-
modern. He compares
pictures. One city with another
as though the tiles don't matter [Delft]
and everything is *Back to the Normal Life*
taking the colour out of the *still* one
Vermeer made, also placing himself [1665]
as *'the artist in his studio'*
the picture with hat and black and white
tiles. Watch for jostling
planes and lines attracting attention
away from the man at the easel. How small [Leiden, 1976]
he looks against the window. His hand [B & W photo]
seems to be brushing something
[Mondrian] away from the blank page.
[Rietveld] Himself perhaps. Maybe
he is making
his mark on history.

II 'Paraplu'

Now we are looking at a 'vacant lot'
(not people but rubble) on a corner
with a concrete wall. Houses
on the edge flecked with snow.
The road's been saltpetred. It takes you
[Delft, 1652] back to a bend Fabritius might have painted. [*vanitas*]
Not a bomb site exactly, but the van could be,
it seems so focused, and what was tree
is a stick in a circle of earth. A man
walks under an umbrella. The artist [Jan de Baenstraat
maybe. Two children also. den Haag, 1983]
'Hanneke and Janneke' the childhood song
making the scene
audible: '*en de klompjes gingen klik klak klip*
en de regen zong van tik tak tik
onder moeder's paraplu'
all part of the everyday *Normal Life* journey
back from earlier landscapes
to a good site (sight)
for the '*artist and his studio*'; [Vermeer]

Meditations on Painters

I 'From Picasso'

Every time it's a leap
not knowing
whether you'll land
in your intentions.
A few sweeps
an idea. Two holes
and you've got a face.
Think of it.
Two strokes to brush
complexity.
It doesn't have to be
real. Years pass, centuries
and the likeness was not
important. But the woman
was most certainly
beautiful.

II 'From Matisse'

Something about light / ness
and spring never suspecting
other seasons might follow.
All a deception of course
there was effort hidden
under hats, magnified
in peasant blouses, behind
latticework. You can't live
in a house that's too tidy.
You've got to get out
to the jungle. Catch music
in blue branches. A seduction
naked cut-outs might achieve.
Forget colour. Only your skin
will express that purity of sky,
those nuances of landscape.

III 'From Picasso: fish-hat'

The renaissance invented
noses. Afterwards reality
went to the devil. A bogey
to frighten children. Miracles
don't exist. You start with an egg
and end with a portrait.
Simple and simply a search.
Beauty has nothing on it. Look
how the woman rubs her hands.
Her eyes turn up. Already
she savours the fish. Any moment
now the plate will rise
to the bait.

IV 'From Picasso: simply'

Ideas are points
of departure. A train
might leave as readily.
Just something that comes
and goes. You set to work
and in no time it begins.
A page, a line, a garden
with rain. Searching
doesn't bring rainbows.
All you have to do is look
in the mirror where everything is
already different. You
give yourself trouble, tear
your hair out, bite your nails,
and it all ends
up / in a bunch of flowers
picked among weeds.

Fate of a Dove

The painting by Joseph Wright of Derby

In the eighteenth century room a boy
is getting the birdcage down
on the canvas. It is *an experiment*
on a bird in the air / pump. Time [1768]
has a hand in it. The audience doesn't
know. They are detached (amazed,
distraught), the way the conjuror holds
his arm ready to let air in
to the jar where the bird waits.
Everything is calm. Even the moon
adds a touch of chiaroscuro (mystery
and science), excitement at the light
pinpointing the darkness.
Breaths are caught. Finally
the hand pushes down in the glow
of the lamp and the bird
flutters (among inaudible sighs)
right in the middle
of the Tate Gallery.

Elizabeth 1 (1533-1603) Detail

For Dorothy Howie

Even the carry–bag was marvellous. Much
travelled and all the way from the National
Portrait Gallery with *Elisabet D.G. Angliae*
Franciae, et Hirbeniae, Regina, a portrait
inside a catalogue by a compatriot. Marcus Gheeraerts
(the younger) 1592. I ironed out the wrinkles
with brown paper the way my mother taught me,
and the collar sprung back in starched folds
each a cathedral window arched and spun with stories
caught in fans round that magnificent neck. Imagine
the lace-makers. How many went blind (or mad)
who did the washing, arranged those folded wings
not to take flight from all that stiff upbearing
(see how the vein throbs in the temple)
into the lightning sky.

Proustian

For Robin Hooper

I saw you walking
down Wynyard Street in your black
blouse spreading silk
billows of pink and mauve
flowers and fans so like the box
my mother had on the dresser
for make-up when I was five.
That was *Coty* and she died
I remember the wind fanned the morning
street serenely / breathed
light and memory in slats
the sun danced through / the gate
swinging (beside the shadows)
on haunting syllables
of fragments.

Peace Poem

For Tu Neill

The boy is practising his skills
around the dinner table. He's learning
[Tuataroa] languages. *'Yo soy hombre* [I am a man of the long morning]
de la albarada larga. Mon frére [Te Ao Huri]
tout bouleverse le monde.' [14 July]
Guests speak in many tongues also
sparring for possession. His own [Maori]
[Gaelic] are not available. Insufficient numbers
the Head says but our hearts listen
for the menace of hooves. Latin
is alive and well and the cane
a matter of tradition. Sentences
break up in fear to wound the soul
and memory begins its dark journey
grieving the language of loss. *'Je t'aime'*
you smile to embrace us, 'but how
do I say "I detest"'. The words cut
the wind harrying the dark on the edge of sky.

Recipe for Peace

Take a handful of seeds
anti-nuclear will do
or anti-pollution for a start
and scatter them around
on your journeys (to work
to school, to friends) anywhere
is fertile. Sprinkle carefully
with words like water, cupping
the raindrops to nourish
the plants as they sprout. Tears
also may be used for growing
and the spittle of despair. Fertilise
with friendship, rallies, singing.
Candles are said to breathe warmth
in winter and the waving of banners
cool air in the heat. Your methods
will vary according to climate
but wherever you plant
flowers will reach for the light.
Only mushrooms thrive
on darkness.

Amanita

A modern day variation of 'the tree of life' story

and the leaves of the tree were for
the healing of the nations
(Revelation 22:1-2)

The glow that spread from the radiant fiery mushroom tree high in the sky, spread down far and wide and into the hidden and mysterious depths of the earth from where it polluted the vital sap of life, which, ascending through the trunk to the head of the poisonous growth, becomes the evil potion of death. In Hiroshima, Nagasaki, Arizona, Kurtachov and Moruroa, the Great Earth Tree from whom all things derive their sustenance and in whose magnificent crown we saw the great unfolding of our potential wholeness, withered and her charred body became a shadow whose poison seeps daily into the sea where fish float belly up. And at the end of time, now, the mushroom swells higher and higher into the sky and more often and covers the sun which it covets and burns up the moon and the stars. And the light is no more, only the burning heat of day. And the fruits of the earth shrivel and the water in the sea burns dry. And there is only darkness and everything that lives dies and the music of the wind that draws all creatures to its heart ceases and the pain lasts for a long long time.

Signal Yellow

The ginger in flower
is what you notice
first all yellow
the gorse up
everywhere
the yellow
brushes on the wattle
along the roadside
as you come round
the bend following
the line of water
you run across
the fog lifting the hills
in the distance almost
yellow.

Track with Tide Coming In

For Susanna and Duncan Stuart

IV 'Paikea Bay'

How / at the just moment everything
conspires against you going
further.
Here is a cleft in the rocks.
The tide smashes, churns and runs
back again to come leaping
up / higher / spitting at you
clinging to the scared (scarred) rock.
A cloud bursts and you ask
who weeps for whom or why —
the sea, the sky, the rock
weeping ?
and as suddenly the warmth again
on the skin as you're over
the crevice and back down
from the jagged leap
to smooth stone
beached
and summer in brittle ochre grass
danthonia & harestail and the great
bleached spiders loping along
in the bowled over wind as it stirs up
the sand skimming across the dunes
and blusters over the cliff
into the boiling frenzy
at the world's edge.
Also Pohuehue Mesembry anthenium
(so the book says) and an interesting
mix, or coastal ice
plant in sharp bright colours.

V 'Home, writing'

There are so many things
the poem can't do.
Where for example in this note
book scribble & drawing
these cryptic messages for later
is the smell of salt & sea
weed & the wind & the dry
grass waving from up the hills?

How now among the Saturday lawn
mowers to re-create the silence
of cobalt viridian green
under the breaking wave?

Northern Building Society Office Showing Police Headquarters, Auckland

If I told you corner of Grey
and Mayoral Drive just opposite
the *Carpenter's Arms* and left
of Cook Street where the markets are
you'd still have no idea
how this building shapes
itself squarely and not too tall
in the lee of the nineteenth century
tower telling you it's three o'clock
and the fountain tumbles over the green
copper slate brighter than summer
pollard showing off in the mirror
glass.
The only worry is the way
the sun reflects what you don't want
to see this blue day –
a concrete cloud.

Chance Meeting

Take the toys
away
from the boys

Hiroshima Day

On my way to *Disorderly Conduct*
a launching of duck & worth(y) words
(a novel, otherwise) with light
refreshments
and drinks in the *Birdcage*
I encounter a young buck
springing to life
on his sky blue Suzuki
(GS450) on the corner.
I watch his legs
press & caress the wide body
and something
stirs
he smiles
under his sky blue
11 Novastar helmet
and I smile watching
his legs, his arms, the way
he bounces and watches
me smiling
and I think Orphée has come
riding right out of a Cocteau
movie, but the lights go green
and he takes off
in another direction
entirely.

[such 'power between
his thighs']

[such an ache /
a thudding ache I press
my legs]

The Poem as Dirt (or How About the Holocaust as Tourist Attraction)

No use writing (you say)
about clouds lonelier than horizons
passing your life by
in straight lines. Forget willows
bending to stroke themselves
in water. Basho's long dead. Breathe
into the real (you say) — the fast track
concentration of crowds belching
to Krakov in tourist buses.
BELSEN WAS A GAS says the wall
round the local synagogue. What
about the holocaust? Make for attraction,
visit the site for the film, feel [Schindler's List]
the gasp of recognition. Cry a little
and recover at 'Ariel'. Good coffee
and excellent treats. Clouds of course
and fancy. Prospero himself
coming to look. Nothing to cross
the boundaries of taste. T shirts, yes
and *'Hitler's European Tours'.* Entertainment
buses turning up good business.
Poems might turn away
and weep.

JOURNEY

You'd suppose the hill
would have a name but there is
no indication on the street
map or road directory
but you know by looking
it's historic it has something
to say. I'm on the corner
blue skies and two flags
flying also a steeple.
Mt Eden landscape
for painters   a brent wong
sky and a binney hill

And there suddenly on the left
the sky sullen grey
frowning low over the harbour
Rangitoto in a sheen
of mist.

I'm cruising at 40
I go on   past   the coca-cola truck

Norfolk pines
and a race course
a lot of cloud
SEACRAFT on a roof
Ellerslie/Penrose

/ going home

Mt Victoria coming up dead
ahead / steers under a tree

white head
red body
green tree

so much for wheelbarrows
william carlos

pylons / glass
and fletcher's yellow belly
belching out the H_2SO_4

oil of vitriol.

and a red train
two carriages with yellow
back / 4692
here the sky
still wong and dry

father fletcher everywhere
smoke, steam
and chimneys
everywhere

we buy we sell we trade
VACANT
BOILERMAKERS
vacant boilermakers ?

And there's Mt Wellington
miserable in the shade
and the sun-less-ness
they've quarried most of her
away / towed her away like
the old V8 on the back
of a truck slowly
down the road

CLEARWAY 4pm-6pm
NO RIGHT TURN
CITIZEN'S ADVICE BUREAU.

We are 1-5 Te Rakau Drive.
A woman crosses against
the lights
at the bus-stop
maybe 20 people.

Poplars beginning to lose
their leaves in a row
the shorn lawn
of a very private school
made public
no fences
showing off
we are into exclusive real
estate / Neil Housing /
corporate buying
corporate rape.

TIP TOP

you could write a poem
about the cars on the road
all in their lanes going
places / write all their names
and
    there's a SMASH / right on
the motorway a dead-on
collision

It's a bore
all these cars
piled
up here

HIACE van and would you believe
a tractor? the lights are green
and all the way now into green
green country
and the green grass grew
all around all around
and the green grass grew

And here's the hill.
It's got a windswept ti tree
growth right on the ridge of it
like a bad haircut
shorn the hawthorn hedge. Too
many gaps. Historic country
you'd think looking at water
tanks one tree and yellow
oh so paintable grass,
I've climbed the hill and down
below is *CABLE PRICE.*

ESCORT CORTINA 2000
LANCER EX
FIAT 12 something *8*
MITSUBISHI TREDIA
GLS / CELESTE XL
someone is *HEMI*
powered, poor Baxter
and everywhere *GLX*
GLX gluxs gluck gluck
and does it
bring happiness

The sun's come out
but factories are pouring
clouds in the sky

and everywhere there's real
estate for sale / unreal
exclusive real estate
FOR SALE

a stand of Australian gums
three near the manse

A man on a roof fixing
tiles with a bucket
*(there's a hole in my bucket
dear Charley, dear Charley)*

a girl on a bike
with a red knapsack
GIVE WAY
PETROL OPEN EVERY DAY

special tomatoes on the corner
where four roads meet.

This was a paddock
(yesterday)
now it is black
scraped and scratched
(earth)
a hundred gulls rest
on the waves
(volcanic country).

I'm going home.

not for long
they're bulldozing
(dozing?) it / scraping it
off like lice in old times.

*Where are you headed ?
Where are you going ?
Where have you been ?
I'm going home.*

and at the corner here
at Fortune's Road / you can
buy a *VAUXHALL* for a fortune
a *BEDFORD,* a *HOLDEN*
and 'NIGHT MUST FALL'
plays at the little theatre

a *MERCEDES* with too much
chrome.

en morgen is er niets.

Where are we heading?
Where are we going?
Where are you heading?
I'm going home.

Where have you been
all the day Billy Boy?

I don't know where
you're headed
but I'm going
home.

Winter

For Elly Guthrie

Years pass, days,
a few hours can change
the world. [6 August 1945]
Think of Hiroshima.
Last
we were walking together
for other upheavals
massed in
waves of placards:
'NO TOUR' 'BIKO'. [winter, 1981]
The children no more
than maybe six. Now they gather
half a century between them
and we like that ending
in novels. Older, eyes sometimes [Orwell's *1984*]
avoiding the fire.

Those who are dead
speak to us.
Those who are gone
speak to us from the stars
the sun in the wind
through branches
lifting
a requiem of loss.

Age

A new month
and the start of summer
but the same old bones
reluctant
into the aching
sea-blue
dawn.

Index